MICROSOFT® *Quick* REFERENCE

MS-DOS®
BATCH FILES

Second Edition

W9-BYH-979

INCLUDES
DOS 5

Microsoft
P R E S S

KRIS JAMSA

PUBLISHED BY
Microsoft Press
A Division of Microsoft Corporation
One Microsoft Way
Redmond, Washington 98052-6399

Library of Congress Cataloging-in-Publication Data
Jamsa, Kris A.
    MS-DOS batch files / Kris A. Jamsa. —2nd ed.
    p.   cm.—(Microsoft quick reference)
    Includes index.
    1. MS-DOS (Computer operating system) 2. File management
(Computer science) 3. Electronic data processing—Batch processing.
I. Title. II. Series.
QA76.76.063J34   1991   005.4'46—dc20   90-27189
ISBN 1-55615-338-4

Printed and bound in the United States of America.

1 2 3 4 5 6 7 8 9 RARA 4 3 2 1

Distributed to the book trade in Canada by Macmillan of Canada,
a division of Canada Publishing Corporation.

Distributed to the book trade outside the United States and Canada by
Penguin Books Ltd.

Penguin Books Ltd., Harmondsworth, Middlesex, England

Penguin Books Australia Ltd., Ringwood, Victoria, Australia

Penguin Books N.Z. Ltd., 182-190 Wairau Road, Auckland 10, New
Zealand

British Cataloging-in-Publication Data available

Acquisitions Editor: Dean Holmes
Project Editor: Editorial Services of New England, Inc.
Technical Editor: Jim Johnson

Contents

Introduction

For years, experienced users of the MS-DOS disk operating system have found that DOS batch files save them time and keystrokes. Put simply, a DOS batch file is a file that contains DOS commands. When you type the name of a batch file at the DOS prompt, DOS executes the commands that the batch file contains. (This book will use the hard-disk drive default prompt C>.) Although many users employ simple batch files on a daily basis, abbreviating a series of commonly used commands, most users fail to take full advantage of the potential that batch files offer.

Until now, the majority of books on batch processing largely focused on non-batch-related DOS commands. This book, however, sticks to its topic. Users new to DOS batch files can begin with the basics. Those who have used simple batch files will learn how to repeat commands and how to branch from one location in a batch file to another. Experienced batch-file users will learn how to add color and line-drawing characters to the screen display generated by their batch files.

Although the DOS batch commands are quite powerful, the commands still don't provide you with all the capabilities you need to get the most from your batch files. This quick reference guide teaches you how to create simple programs, using DEBUG, that let your batch files prompt the user for a Y (yes) or N (no) response, how to test to see if a specific function key has been pressed, and even how to use the direction keys to move menu options. These programs take only minutes to create. You don't need any special programming languages—all you need is DOS!

This book also teaches you how to have your batch file ask the user for information and then how to read and use the information provided. For years, users have wanted these capabilities: This quick reference shows you how you can have them.

If you are using MS-DOS version 5.0, this guide teaches you how to create macro definitions using the DOSKEY command. A macro is similiar to a DOS batch file in that it contains the names of one or more commands you can execute by simply typing the macro name. Unlike DOS batch files, macros reside in your computer's fast electronic RAM (random-access memory) instead of on disks. If you are using DOS 5, the knowledge of the DOSKEY command will make you immediately more productive.

You don't have to be an expert to use this guide. Any DOS user can easily follow the examples. Learning how to create and use batch files might just be the most productive time you spend at your computer—because it will save you time whenever you use your computer.

PART I

Getting Started with Batch Files

UNDERSTANDING BATCH-FILE PROCESSING

The number of DOS commands now exceeds 80. Most of us, however, use only a small group of DOS commands, such as COPY, REN, DEL, TYPE, DISKCOPY, and FORMAT—and possibly the subdirectory commands. Therefore, we probably won't recall the format for many other DOS commands, let alone their command-line switches.

To accomplish specific tasks such as selecting a specific directory and running a word processor, novice users often have to perform a series of commands. As the amount of typing that a user must perform increases, so too does the possibility of error. An error can be the omission of a critical command, or it can be a typographical error.

To decrease the likelihood of error and to simplify your use of DOS, DOS supports batch files. A batch file is a file you create that contains one or more DOS commands. To execute all the commands within a batch file, a user simply types the name of the batch file at a DOS prompt and presses the Enter key, exactly as if the batch file were a single DOS command. When DOS encounters the batch file, DOS executes all the batch commands, starting with the first command and working toward the last.

To begin, let's examine a simple batch file, named TIMEDATE.BAT, that contains three basic DOS commands:

```
CLS
TIME
DATE
```

3

You will create this batch file later; for now, we'll simply discuss how it works.

CLS clears the screen display. TIME displays the current time and prompts the user to enter a new time. DATE displays the current date and prompts the user to enter a new date.

Notice the BAT filename extension. File extensions can describe the type of information a file contains. In the case of TIMEDATE.BAT, the BAT extension tells the user, as well as DOS, that the file is a batch file. To run the batch file, you would type the name of the batch file at the DOS prompt and then press the Enter key, as follows:

```
C> TIMEDATE
```

When DOS encounters the name of the batch file, DOS opens the batch file and executes the first command in the file—in this case, the CLS command. After CLS completes execution, DOS executes the next command in the batch file—the TIME command. At this point, DOS displays the following:

```
C> TIME
Current time is 11:26:46.03a
Enter new time:
```

You would now type the correct time and press the Enter key, or you would press Enter to leave the time unchanged. (Note: DOS releases prior to version 4.0 do not support the 12-hour clock. Such versions would not display an *a*, as shown above, for A.M. This book revision is based on DOS 5; exceptions are noted.) After TIME completes execution, DOS executes the DATE command and displays the following:

```
C> DATE
Current date is Sat 05-11-1991
Enter new date (mm-dd-yy):
```

You would now type the correct date and press Enter, or you would press Enter to leave the date unchanged. When the DATE command completes execution, DOS searches for the next command in the batch file. Because no other commands exist, the batch file completes execution and DOS displays its prompt.

Let's examine another batch file, named DISKINFO.BAT, that contains three DOS commands:

```
VOL
CHKDSK
DIR
```

To execute the commands in this file, which display specifics about the default drive, you would type the name of the batch file and press Enter:

```
C> DISKINFO
```

If DOS displays the message *Bad command or file name* when you execute this batch file, it signifies that DOS could not locate the external command, CHKDSK.COM. Remember: External commands must reside on the floppy disk or in the current drive or be accessible via the command path defined by the DOS command PATH.

A Note for OS/2 Users

Batch files are not unique to DOS. OS/2 batch files behave in the same manner as DOS batch files. The difference between DOS and OS/2 batch files is simply naming. OS/2 real mode allows you to execute DOS commands and DOS batch files with the extension BAT. In OS/2 protected mode, however, batch files have the extension CMD. CMD, in this case, is short for command. Assuming you are using OS/2 protected mode, you can create a batch file, named TIMEDATE.CMD, that contains three DOS commands: CLS, TIME, and DATE.

As before, to run the batch file, type its filename at the OS/2 prompt and then press the Enter key:

```
[C:\] TIMEDATE
```

When OS/2 encounters the batch file, OS/2 executes the batch-file commands, starting with the first command and working toward the last.

ADVANTAGES BATCH FILES PROVIDE

Regardless of whether you are using DOS or OS/2, batch files save you time, reduce your keystrokes and errors, and simplify the execution of difficult commands. Let's look at several batch-file examples that show you how.

Saving Time with Batch Files

Assume that each morning you must run four inventory-control programs. The first program, CALCINV.EXE, calculates your current product inventory. The second, SORTINV.EXE, sorts the inventory by quantity on hand. The third, PRINTINV.EXE, prints listings of inventory quantities on hand. The fourth, ORDERINV.EXE, generates purchase orders for items that need to be stocked.

To run these four programs, you must type in the name of the first program, press the Enter key, and wait for the program to complete execution before repeating these steps for the remaining programs. You might spend a considerable amount of time sitting at the keyboard and waiting for each program to complete execution.

These commands are excellent candidates for a batch file. In this case, you might name the batch file GETINV.BAT. This file contains the following four commands: CALCINV, SORTINV, PRINTINV, and ORDERINV.

When you type the name of the batch file and press Enter, DOS sequentially executes the four commands for you:

```
C> GETINV

C> CALCINV

C> SORTINV

C> PRINTINV

C> ORDERINV
```

Because DOS executes the commands for you automatically, you are free to perform other tasks away from your computer. In this way, using a batch file can save considerable time each day.

Saving Keystrokes and Reducing Errors with Batch Files

Because batch files allow you to execute multiple commands by entering one command name, they reduce the number of keystrokes a user must enter, which directly reduces the possibility of error. In the previous example, executing the batch file GETINV.BAT not only reduced the number of keystrokes but also eliminated the possibility of the user executing a command in the wrong order, typing a command incorrectly, or omitting a command.

Simplifying Command Execution

Each one of us was new to DOS at one time. Most of us can remember the intimidation we felt when we issued our first DOS commands. Batch files help to minimize this intimidation by reducing the number of difficult commands that a new user must remember and successfully execute. For example, most users keep their word processing files in a unique subdirectory. To run the word processor, the user must first select the correct subdirectory by using the CHDIR (Change Directory) command and then select the word processor. In the case of Microsoft Word, for example, the sequence of commands becomes:

```
C> CHDIR \WORD
C> WORD
```

Whether you are a new user or an experienced user helping a beginner, you might consider creating a batch file, named DOWORD.BAT, that contains both commands. The fewer commands a new user must memorize, the more comfortable the new user will feel with the computer. As a result, the new user will learn faster.

NAMING YOUR BATCH FILES

You should always try to give meaningful filenames to every file that you create on your disk. Batch files are no exception. Batch files must have the BAT extension under DOS and the CMD extension under OS/2. As a result, you have only the eight-character filename to distinguish one batch file from another. The name of the batch file should clearly explain the processing that the batch file performs. For example, earlier we examined the batch file TIMEDATE.BAT, which set your system's time and date; and in our inventory example, the batch file was GETINV.BAT. Both of these batch-file names explain the processing the files perform. Although naming a batch file X.BAT or Z.BAT is easy, neither name describes what the batch file does. A few days after you create such a batch file, you probably won't recall its function.

Do not give a batch file the same name as a DOS internal command or external command. Each time you type a command at the DOS prompt, DOS first checks to see if your command is an internal command (such as CLS, DATE, or TIME), which DOS keeps in memory at all times. If your command is an internal command, DOS executes it (instead of the batch-file command). Otherwise, DOS tests to see if the command is an external command in the current directory. An external DOS command (such as DISKCOPY or FORMAT) is a command that resides on disk. If your command is not an internal command in memory or an external command on disk, DOS tests to see if your command corresponds to a DOS batch file. DOS and OS/2 will execute batch files only if no matching internal or external command exists in the current drive and directory. If you give your batch file the same name as that of a DOS command, DOS will never execute the batch file. For example, if your batch file is named TIME.BAT, DOS will locate the DOS command TIME and then execute only the DOS command.

CREATING YOUR BATCH FILES

The method you choose to create batch files can vary, depending on their length. For short batch files, the simplest
and fastest method is to copy the batch file from the keyboard. To do so, you perform a copy operation using CON
(the device name for the keyboard) as the source of your
batch file's input. In this case, we will create the batch file
TIMEDATE.BAT, which sets the system time and date. To
begin the batch-file copy operation, type the following
command at the DOS prompt:

`C> COPY CON TIMEDATE.BAT`

DOS will perform a copy operation using the COPY command. In this case, the source of the data to copy is the keyboard. The target of the copy operation is the batch file
TIMEDATE.BAT. When you press the Enter key to begin
the copy operation, DOS places the cursor at the start of
the line following the command. At this point, DOS is waiting for the first line of input. Type the command *TIME*,
which is the first batch-file command, and press Enter:

```
C> COPY CON TIMEDATE.BAT
TIME
```

Next, type the command DATE and press Enter:

```
C> COPY CON TIMEDATE.BAT
TIME
DATE
```

The DATE command is the last command in the batch file.
You must tell DOS that you have no more input for the
file. To do so, press the F6 (end-of-file) function key and
then press Enter. DOS will display the characters ^Z at the
bottom of your batch file. (Caution: Do not press Shift-8 to
create the caret. You can, however, hold down the Control
[Ctrl] key and press Z.) The ^Z characters, pronounced
Control Z, indicate the end of the file to DOS. When you
press Enter following ^Z, you inform DOS that you have

completed the file copy operation. As a result, DOS creates
the batch file and displays the following:

```
C> COPY CON TIMEDATE.BAT
TIME
DATE
^Z
     1 File(s) copied
C>
```

To execute this batch file, type TIMEDATE:

```
C> TIMEDATE
```

When you press Enter, DOS executes the TIME command
and then the DATE command.

Using the COPY CON technique, create a batch file,
named DISKINFO.BAT, that contains the commands
VOL, CHKDSK, and DIR. As before, type the COPY command line, using the CON device name as your input
source, and press Enter:

```
C> COPY CON DISKINFO.BAT
```

Next, type each batch-file command, pressing Enter after
each command name:

```
C> COPY CON DISKINFO.BAT
VOL
CHKDSK
DIR
```

To tell DOS you're finished entering commands, press the
F6 key and then press Enter. DOS creates the batch file
and tells you that one file has been copied:

```
C> COPY CON DISKINFO.BAT
VOL
CHKDSK
DIR
^Z
     1 File(s) copied

C>
```

To create small batch files from the keyboard, follow
these steps:

1. Issue a COPY command using CON as the source and
   using a meaningful name for the batch file as the target.
   Then press Enter. For example:

   C> COPY CON DATEPRNT.BAT

2. Type one batch-file command at a time, and press Enter
   after each command.

3. After typing the last batch-file command, press the F6 key
   and then press Enter. (F6 signals the end of the file to DOS.)

Creating Larger Batch Files

As your batch files get larger, you will want to use a word
processor, EDIT (MS-DOS version 5.0's full-screen editor), or the Edlin line editor that previous versions of DOS
provided. If you use a word processor, be sure that you
save the file in nondocument (ASCII) mode. As you might
have observed, word processors allow you to format text
within a letter or report by aligning paragraphs, centering
text, or highlighting specific text. To perform these tasks,
word processors place embedded characters within your
file. Although these embedded characters are meaningful
to the word processor, DOS does not understand them. If
these characters appear in your batch files, they cause errors. If you save your word-processing files in ASCII
mode, the word processor will not embed these characters.

Creating a Batch File with Edlin

If you perform a directory listing of the files in your DOS
directory (on hard-disk systems) or on your DOS disk
(on floppy-disk systems), you will see that DOS provides
the file EDLIN.EXE, as follows. (In releases prior to
MS-DOS version 5.0, the name is EDLIN.COM.)

```
C:\DOS> DIR EDLIN.EXE

 Volume in drive C is DOS 5
 Volume Serial Number is 3A2F-18E9
 Directory of  C:\DOS
```

```
EDLIN    EXE      12578 12-13-90   4:09a
       1 File(s)        12578 bytes
                     21113945 bytes free
```

Edlin is a line editor (meaning you can work with only one line at a time) that allows you to create and change files. To understand how Edlin works, let's use it to create a batch file, named SHORTDIR.BAT, that contains the commands CLS and DIR /W.

To begin, run Edlin from the DOS prompt and specify the file to edit. (You must specify a filename in your Edlin command line.) In this case, your command line is:

```
C> EDLIN SHORTDIR.BAT
```

When you press Enter, Edlin displays:

```
C> EDLIN SHORTDIR.BAT
New file
*
```

The asterisk symbol (*) is the Edlin prompt. Edlin supports several single-letter commands. For our purposes, we will use only a few of these commands. (For a complete discussion of Edlin, refer to your DOS user's manual.)

To insert a command into a batch file, you must issue the Edlin insert command, I, and press Enter:

```
C> EDLIN SHORTDIR.BAT
New file
*I
        1:*
```

Edlin prompts you to enter the first line of the batch file. Type *CLS* and press Enter:

```
C> EDLIN SHORTDIR.BAT
New file
*I
        1:* CLS
        2:*
```

Edlin now prompts you for the second line. Type *DIR /W* and press Enter:

```
C> EDLIN SHORTDIR.BAT
New file
```

```
*I
        1:* CLS
        2:* DIR /W
```

Because only two lines are required for this batch file, you must tell Edlin you've finished inserting text. To do so, hold down the key labeled Ctrl and press the C key. When you press Ctrl-C, Edlin exits the insert mode and displays its prompt, as follows:

```
C> EDLIN SHORTDIR.BAT
New file
*I
        1:* CLS
        2:* DIR /W
        3:* ^C
*
```

To save the file, exiting Edlin and returning to DOS, enter the Edlin end command, E, and press Enter:

```
C> EDLIN SHORTDIR.BAT
New file
*I
        1:* CLS
        2:* DIR /W
        3:* ^C
*E

C>
```

To run your newly created batch file, type *SHORTDIR*:

```
C> SHORTDIR
```

and press Enter. DOS clears the screen and displays your directory listing with filename columns across the screen (as directed by the /W switch).

As discussed, Edlin allows you to change an existing file. Now let's change the file SHORTDIR.BAT so that DOS displays only those files with the extension EXE. As before, type *EDLIN* and specify the filename:

```
C> EDLIN SHORTDIR.BAT
```

Because the file SHORTDIR.BAT already exists, Edlin displays the following message:

```
C> EDLIN SHORTDIR.BAT
End of input file
*
```

In this case, Edlin is telling you that it has read the entire
file and that it is ready to edit. When you type the numeral
1 at the Edlin prompt and press Enter, Edlin displays the
first line in the file:

```
C> EDLIN SHORTDIR.BAT
End of input file
*1
        1:* CLS
        1:*
```

The second *1:** that appears on your screen is Edlin's
prompt for you to change line 1. If you want to leave line 1
unchanged, press Enter; otherwise, type the new text for
line 1. For now, leave line 1 unchanged (by pressing Enter):

```
C> EDLIN SHORTDIR.BAT
End of input file
*1
        1:* CLS
        1:*
*
```

At the Edlin prompt, type the numeral *2* and press Enter.
Edlin displays the contents of line 2, allowing you to
change it:

```
C> EDLIN SHORTDIR.BAT
End of input file
*1
        1:* CLS
        1:*
*2
        2:* DIR /W
        2:*
```

In this case, you need to change line 2 from *DIR /W* to
DIR *.EXE /W. Type the new line and press Enter:

```
C> EDLIN SHORTDIR.BAT
End of input file
*1
        1:* CLS
        1:*
```

```
*2
        2:* DIR /W
        2:* DIR *.EXE /W
*
```

Again, by entering the Edlin end command, E, and pressing Enter, you save the updated file contents and exit to
DOS:

```
C> EDLIN SHORTDIR.BAT
End of input file
*1
        1:* CLS
        1:*
*2
        2:* DIR /W
        2:* DIR *.EXE /W
*E

C>
```

If you now run the batch file, DOS clears the screen and
displays only those files with the extension EXE.

If you want to stop editing the file without saving any
changes, use the Edlin quit command, Q. When you issue
the command, Edlin responds with:

```
Abort edit (Y/N)?
```

If you type Y (for yes) and press Enter, Edlin ignores your
edits, exits to DOS, and leaves the file unchanged. If you type
N (for no) and press Enter, Edlin continues the editing session.

Later in this reference, we will use Edlin to create batch
files that change your screen settings and to assign commonly used DOS commands to the function keys on your
keyboard. We will also continue our discussion of DOS
batch files and batch-file commands. But first, let's take a
look at a simple batch file that you might want to use on a
daily basis.

Using Edlin, let's create another batch file, named
SORTDIR.BAT, that contains the command to print a
sorted listing of your files:

```
C> EDLIN SORTDIR.BAT
New file
*I
```

```
    1:* DIR | SORT > PRN
    2:* ^C
*E

C>
```

Creating a Batch File with EDIT

MS-DOS version 5.0 includes a full-screen text editor, called EDIT. If you perform a directory listing of the files in your DOS directory (on hard-disk systems) or on your DOS disk (on floppy-disk systems), you will see that DOS provides the file EDIT.COM, as follows:

```
C:\DOS> DIR EDIT.COM

 Volume in drive C is DOS 5
 Volume Serial Number is 3160-12D7
 Directory of C:\DOS

EDIT      COM       413 12-13-90    4:09a
        1 file(s)         413 bytes
                    21690176 bytes free
```

EDIT is a full-screen editor (meaning EDIT lets you use the entire screen) that allows you to create and change files. To understand how EDIT works, let's use it to create a batch file named SHORTDIR.BAT, which contains the commands CLS and DIR /W.

To begin, run EDIT from the DOS prompt and specify the name of the file to edit. (If you do not specify a file name, you can specify one later when you save the file on disk.) For this example, your command line is:

```
C> EDIT SHORTDIR.BAT
```

When you press Enter, EDIT displays the screen in Figure 1.

The blinking underscore in the upper left corner is the cursor—the place characters appear as you type them. Centered above the area you type in is the name of the file, SHORTDIR.BAT. (If you did not specify a filename on the command line, the word *Untitled* would appear there.) Above and left of the filename are the four drop-down menus you use to issue commands to EDIT. For this

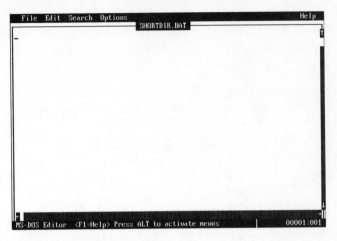

Figure 1. *The EDIT screen.*

example, we will only use a couple of menu commands.
(For a complete discussion of EDIT, refer to your DOS
user's manual.)

To create SHORTDIR.BAT, type in the following commands, pressing Enter at the end of each line:

```
CLS
DIR /W
```

If you make a typing mistake, use the Backspace key until
you erase the error and then retype the rest of the line. If
the cursor is on another line, use the arrow keys to move
the cursor to the line containing the error, and then use the
backspace key to correct the problem.

To save SHORTDIR.BAT on disk, drop down the File
menu by first pressing the Alt key and then pressing the
F key. Next, choose the File menu's Save command by
pressing S.

(If you did not specify a filename when you started EDIT,
EDIT displays a dialog box that asks you to enter the name
of the file. Simply type *SHORTDIR.BAT* and press Enter to
name and save the file.)

Before you can try out the batch file, you must quit the
EDIT program and return to the DOS prompt. To do this,

press Alt, F (to drop down the File menu), and then X (to
choose the File menu's Exit command).

To run your newly created batch file, type *SHORTDIR*:

C>`SHORTDIR`

and press Enter. DOS clears the screen and displays your
directory listing with filename columns across the screen
(as directed by the /W switch).

EDIT also allows you to change an existing file. Let's
change SHORTDIR.BAT so that DOS displays only those
files with the extension EXE. As before, type EDIT and
specify the filename:

C>`EDIT SHORTDIR.BAT`

Because the file already exists, EDIT displays the contents
of the file in its window, exactly as you typed it in.

To change the file, move the cursor to the line you want to
change, make the change, then save the file again. You
want to add the file filter *.EXE to the second line, so
begin by pressing the down-arrow key to move the cursor
down one line. Next, press the End key to move the cursor
to the end of the line. Next, press the left-arrow key two
times to move the cursor under the /. Finally, type *.*EXE*
followed by one space. The */W* already in the line should
move to the right as you type, and the end result should
look like Figure 2.

(If your batch file differs from Figure 2, make any necessary corrections now.) To save the changed file, press Alt,
F, and then S. Finally, to quit the EDIT program and return
to the DOS prompt, press Alt, F, and then X. Now if you
run the batch file, DOS clears the screen and displays only
those files with the extension EXE.

If you want to stop editing a file in EDIT and return to the
DOS prompt without saving any changes to the file,
choose the File menu's Exit command. When you use the
Exit command without first saving the file (or changes to
an existing file), EDIT displays the dialog box in Figure 3.

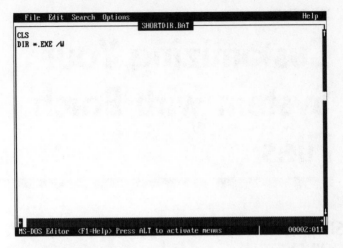

Figure 2. *SHORTDIR.BAT after editing.*

If you choose Yes, EDIT saves any changes you made to
the file before returning to the DOS prompt. This prevents
you from accidently quitting the EDIT program before saving any changes. If you choose No, EDIT does *not* save
any changes you made and returns you to the DOS prompt.
If you choose Cancel, EDIT cancels the Exit command and
returns you to the file, allowing you to continue the editing
session.

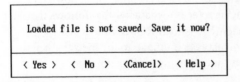

Figure 3. *The Exit dialog box.*

PART II

Customizing Your System with Batch Files

USING BATCH FILES TO CUSTOMIZE YOUR SYSTEM

Many users personalize their systems by changing the DOS prompt. By default, DOS displays the current disk-drive letter followed by the greater-than symbol (>) as its prompt. For example: C>.

Many users also like to display the current directory within the prompt. To do so, users must issue the PROMPT command. If you examine the PROMPT command in the DOS user's manual, you will find that PROMPT supports several unique character combinations called *metacharacters*. In general, a metacharacter is a character that follows the dollar-sign character ($). When PROMPT detects a metacharacter, it displays text unique to the metacharacter. PROMPT supports the following metacharacters:

Metacharacter	Corresponding Text
$$	$ character
$b	I character
$d	Current system date
$e	ASCII escape character
$g	> character
$h	ASCII backspace character

(continued)

continued

Metacharacter	Corresponding Text
$l	< character
$n	Current disk drive
$p	Current disk drive and directory
$q	= character
$t	Current system time
$v	Current DOS version
$_	Carriage return, linefeed

In OS/2 only, the following metacharacters are also supported:

Metacharacter	Corresponding Text
$a	& character
$c	(character
$f	) character
$i	The help line
$s	Insert a leading space

As you can imagine, remembering these metacharacters could be a difficult task. A better alternative is to determine the prompt setting that you want and then to place the corresponding PROMPT command in a batch file named MYPROMPT.BAT. For example, the following command displays the current system date on one line and the current drive and directory two lines below enclosed in brackets:

```
PROMPT $d$_$_[$p]
```

Assuming that you place this command in the batch file MYPROMPT.BAT, executing the batch file results in prompt lines resembling the following:

```
Sat 05-11-1991

[C:\DOS]
```

As you can see, DOS displays the current date, followed by the current directory within open and close brackets. (Note that the brackets, as with other characters not preceded by the $ character, are displayed exactly as entered.) Regardless of the system prompt you choose, most users find that a prompt containing the current drive and directory is very functional. By setting your desired prompt with a DOS batch file, you don't have to remember the PROMPT command line from one day to another or enter it each session.

The first time you issue the PRINT command, DOS installs software in your computer's memory that manages your printer and the files you print, and it lets you include several switches in the command line. (Note: The switches that can take parameters can be specified only when PRINT is first executed.) The switches specify such preferences as the selected printer (normally PRN for parallel printers and COM1 for serial printers); the size of the print queue, from 4 through 32 (by default, DOS will hold 10 files for printing, in a list called a queue); and several switches that determine how much of your computer's time is spent printing files. The following table briefly describes PRINT's switches:

Switch	Function
/B	Specifies the size of the print buffer.
/C	Cancels one or more files in the print queue.
/D	Specifies the target output device.
/M	Specifies the number of clock ticks during which PRINT can retain control of the printer for each time it begins printing.
/Q	Specifies the number of files the print queue can store.
/S	Specifies the print time slice, which controls how often PRINT gains control of the printer.
/T	Cancels all files in the print queue.
/U	Specifies the number of clock ticks that PRINT can wait for the printer to become available.
/P	Prints the files named on this command line.

Most users use PRINT's default settings simply because they don't remember the available switches. In many cases, users can get better performance from their printer and computer by including a few simple switches in the PRINT command. DOS batch files provide you with an easy way to run PRINT with its optimal settings. For most users, the following command line will give the best performance:

```
PRINT /D:PRN /Q:32 /M:64 /U:16 /B:4096
```

If you are using a serial printer connected to the first adapter, change the /D switch to reference COM1:

```
PRINT /D:COM1 /Q:32 /M:64 /U:16 /B:4096
```

In this case, the command installs a queue large enough for 32 files using the /Q switch. The /D switch tells PRINT the device to print to. By including this switch, PRINT suppresses the prompt (*Name of list device [PRN]:*) that PRINT normally displays the first time you run it. The /M switch directs PRINT to retain control of the computer for 64 clock ticks each time it begins printing. The /U switch directs PRINT to retain control for 16 clock ticks while waiting for the printer to become available, if the printer is currently busy.

Lastly, the /B switch sets aside a print buffer of 4096 bytes. PRINT fills this buffer with characters from the file each time it reads from disk. Because this buffer is quite large (the default is 512 bytes), PRINT reduces the number of slow disk-input operations it must perform to print a file. Reducing disk-input operations improves overall system performance. Note that OS/2 supports only the /C, /D, and /T switches.

You might call the batch file PRINTINS.BAT (for Print Install). Although the MYPROMPT.BAT and PRINTINS.BAT batch files are quite simple, both show you how batch files eliminate the burden of remembering difficult commands.

You might be thinking that you would like to issue these commands on a daily basis, or better yet, each time DOS starts. As it turns out, DOS lets you create one special batch file, called AUTOEXEC.BAT, whose contents DOS executes each time you start the system. If you are using OS/2, the operating system executes a similar batch file, called STARTUP.CMD, each time the system starts. AUTOEXEC.BAT and STARTUP.CMD have the same function—to provide a set of commands that automatically execute each time you start the system.

LOOKING AT AUTOEXEC.BAT

Users generally need to execute several DOS commands each time they work with their systems. These commands include PROMPT (which sets your system prompt), PRINT (which installs printer-management software), PATH (which defines the set of subdirectories and disk drives that DOS searches for executable programs), APPEND (which defines the data-file search path), and SET (which defines DOS environment variables), as well as third-party software commands that install memory-resident software programs. If you group these commands into a batch file, you don't have to type these commands each time you start your system.

When DOS starts, it searches the root (uppermost) directory of the boot disk for the batch file AUTOEXEC.BAT. If this file exists, DOS opens it and executes the commands it contains, beginning with the first command in the file and working its way toward the last.

If DOS cannot find AUTOEXEC.BAT in the root directory, DOS instead displays a copyright message and executes the DATE and TIME commands. To better understand this processing, let's take a look at a sample AUTOEXEC.BAT file:

```
PATH C:\DOS
PROMPT $p$g
PRINT /D:LPT1 /Q:32 /M:64 /U:16 /B:4096
```

This batch file contains three commands commonly found in AUTOEXEC.BAT. The first command:

```
PATH C:\DOS
```

defines the command search path. Each time DOS fails to locate a command in the current directory or in the directory specified, DOS checks to see if you have defined a command search path. The DOS command PATH lets you specify a list of one or more subdirectories that DOS searches for executable programs. In this case, if DOS does not locate the specified program, it searches the subdirectory DOS on drive C for the program. Because this subdirectory contains all the external DOS commands, DOS will very likely locate the command. If your disk has other subdirectories that contain commonly used files, PATH lets you include them in the command-file search path by separating each directory with a semicolon, as follows:

```
PATH C:\DOS;C:\UTIL;C:\BIN
```

In this case, if DOS fails to locate a program in the current directory or in the specified directory, DOS begins its search for the program in the subdirectory C:\DOS. If DOS locates the program, DOS executes it. Otherwise, DOS continues searching the directories C:\UTIL and C:\BIN (in that order).

Place only those subdirectories that are likely to contain executable programs into your command search path. Each time DOS uses the command search path, DOS examines every file, in every directory specified in the path, stopping when the file is found. If a subdirectory in the path is not likely to contain an executable program, DOS is wasting time searching the files in that subdirectory.

The second command in this batch file:

```
PROMPT $p$g
```

sets the DOS system prompt to the current drive and directory name, followed by the > symbol. As you change drives or directories, DOS changes your prompt, displaying the current default drive and directory. In this case, assuming that the current directory is the root directory in drive C, your prompt is:

```
C:\>
```

If you use CHDIR (Change Directory) to select the subdirectory DOS, for example, DOS changes your prompt, as follows:

```
C:\> CHDIR \DOS
C:\DOS>
```

If you change the current drive, DOS changes the prompt. For example, here is how the prompt changes when you change the current drive from C to A:

```
C:\DOS> A:
A:\>
```

Most users display the current directory and drive in the system prompt for convenience.

The third command:

```
PRINT /D:LPT1 /Q:32 /M:64 /U:16 /B:4096
```

installs software that DOS uses to manage the files you later print using the DOS command PRINT.

The actual commands that your AUTOEXEC.BAT file contains can vary with the program that you use. If your system does not have a battery-powered clock that stores the system date and time, you need to include the DOS commands DATE and TIME in AUTOEXEC.BAT. Placing DATE and TIME in this batch file will ensure that you are prompted for data to keep your system's date and time correct.

Be especially careful when you change the contents of the AUTOEXEC.BAT file. A good rule to follow is that you never change AUTOEXEC.BAT without first having made a backup copy of the file. To save AUTOEXEC.BAT, copy it to a second file, called AUTOEXEC.SAV, as follows:

```
C> COPY AUTOEXEC.BAT AUTOEXEC.SAV
```

If you should later want to access the previous version of the file, you have it readily available on disk.

AUTOEXEC.BAT *vs* CONFIG.SYS

Many DOS users are confused by the difference between AUTOEXEC.BAT and CONFIG.SYS. AUTOEXEC.BAT is a batch file whose commands DOS executes each time you start your system. CONFIG.SYS, however, is not a batch file. (Remember: DOS batch files must have the filename extension BAT.) Files with the filename extension SYS are operating-system files that perform specific tasks. In the case of CONFIG.SYS, the file contains values that DOS uses to configure itself in memory each time the system starts. Such values include, for example, the BUFFERS= entry (which defines the number of disk buffers DOS uses) and the FILES= entry (which specifies the number of files DOS can have open at one time). The following table briefly describes the CONFIG.SYS entries:

Entry	**Function**
BREAK=	Enables/disables extended Ctrl-Break checking.
BUFFERS=	Specifies the number of disk I/O buffers.
COUNTRY=	Identifies a new country, if country-specific information is available. (New in MS-DOS version 2.1 and in PC-DOS version 3.0)
DEVICE=	Installs a device driver.
DEVICE HIGH=	Specifies that the named DOS device driver should be loaded above 640 K. (New in MS-DOS version 5.0)
DOS=	Sets the area of RAM (above or below 640 KB) into which MS-DOS will load itself. (New in MS-DOS version 5.0)
DRIVPARM=	Specifies block device characteristics. Unique to MS-DOS. (Versions 3.2 and later)
FCBS=	Specifies the number of file control blocks DOS supports for older programs. (Versions 3.0 and later)
FILES=	Specifies the number of files DOS can have open at one time.
INSTALL=	Allows loading of certain DOS commands during CONFIG.SYS processing. (Versions 4.0 and later)
LASTDRIVE=	Specifies the last disk-drive letter that DOS will support. (Versions 3.0 and later)
REM=	Allows comment lines within a CONFIG.SYS file. (Versions 4.0 and later)

(continued)

continued

Entry	Function
SHELL=	Defines a command-line processor other than DOS.
STACKS=	Provides additional stack space for systems encountering too many hardware interrupts at one time. (MS-DOS versions 3.2 and later and PC-DOS versions 3.3 and later)
SWITCHES=	Uses conventional keyboard functions when an extended keyboard is installed. (PC-DOS version 4.0 and later and MS-DOS version 5)

Each time DOS starts, it installs itself in your computer's memory before executing any other commands. During this process, DOS examines the contents of the system file CONFIG.SYS. DOS uses the entries in the CONFIG.SYS file to customize the operating system. If this file does not exist, DOS uses default values.

Only after DOS is completely installed does it check for the existence of the batch file AUTOEXEC.BAT. So, although DOS uses both CONFIG.SYS and AUTOEXEC.BAT during system startup, it uses these files for two distinct purposes and in a specific order.

PART III

Essential Batch Commands and Concepts

SUPPRESSING THE DISPLAY OF BATCH-FILE COMMAND NAMES

By default, each time you execute a batch file, DOS displays the name of each command as it executes. For example, let's look again at the batch file GETINV.BAT, which contains the commands CALCINV, SORTINV, PRINTINV, and ORDERINV.

As you might recall, DOS displays the name of each command as it is executed. As a result, your screen contains the following:

```
C> GETINV

C> CALCINV

C> SORTINV

C> PRINTINV

C> ORDERINV

C>
```

You might not always want DOS to display the names of the batch-file commands as they execute. Your reason for suppressing the command-name display might simply be to reduce screen clutter, or you might not want the user to know the commands that DOS is executing. Depending on your version of DOS, two methods exist to suppress command-name display in batch files. For users of DOS versions 3.3 and later or OS/2, placing the @ character at the start of a command name directs DOS to suppress the command-name display. For example, the batch file VERVOL.BAT displays the current DOS version number as well as the current disk volume label:

```
@VER
@VOL
```

Because both of the batch-file commands (VER and VOL) are preceded by the @ character, DOS does not display the command name. When you run this batch file, DOS displays the current DOS version and disk volume label, as follows:

```
MS-DOS version 5.00

 Volume in drive C is DOS 5
 Volume Serial Number is 3921-18D3

C>
```

Contrast this output with that of VERVOL2.BAT, whose two commands (VER and VOL) do not suppress the command names. When you run this batch file, DOS displays the following:

```
C> VER

MS-DOS version 5.00

C> VOL

 Volume in drive C is DOS 5
 Volume Serial Number is 3921-18D3

C>
```

Remember: To use the @ character within a batch file, you must be using DOS version 3.3 (or later) or OS/2.

For users with older DOS versions, the batch-file command ECHO allows your batch files to suppress command-name display. With older versions of DOS, it is common to place the command ECHO OFF as the first batch-file command. When DOS encounters ECHO OFF, DOS does not display the names of the batch-file commands as they execute. For example, the batch file VER VOL3.BAT uses ECHO OFF, as follows:

```
ECHO OFF
VER
VOL
```

When you run this batch file, DOS displays the following:

```
C> ECHO OFF

MS-DOS version 5.00

 Volume in drive C is DOS 5
 Volume Serial Number is 3921-18D3

C>
```

As you can see, DOS did not display the command names VER and VOL. However, DOS does display the message:

```
C> ECHO OFF
```

If you are using DOS version 3.3 (or later) or OS/2, you can eliminate the ECHO OFF message by preceding the ECHO OFF command with the @ character. If you are using an older version of DOS, consider placing the CLS command in the batch file, immediately following the ECHO OFF command (as shown below), to clear the screen before displaying the output of the VER and VOL commands:

```
ECHO OFF
CLS
VER
VOL
```

Let's assume that this batch file is named VERVOL4.BAT. When you run this batch file, DOS displays the following:

```
MS-DOS version 5.00

 Volume in drive C is DOS 5
 Volume Serial Number is 3921-18D3

C>
```

Later in this reference, we will use the ECHO command extensively within our batch files to write messages to the user, to set the screen colors, and even to redefine keys on your keyboard. For now, however, understand that the ECHO OFF command inhibits the display of batch-file commands when DOS executes a batch file. If, for some reason, you want to display the names of some commands as they execute (we will see why you might want to do this later), the command ECHO ON enables command name display (the DOS default setting). This last version of the VER, VOL batch file, named VERVOL5.BAT, illustrates the use of ECHO ON and ECHO OFF:

```
ECHO OFF
CLS
VER
ECHO ON
VOL
```

When you run this batch file, DOS displays the following:

```
MS-DOS version 5.00

C> VOL

 Volume in drive C is DOS 5
 Volume Serial Number is 3921-18D3

C>
```

As you can see, DOS suppressed the display of the command name for the CLS, VER, and ECHO ON commands. After the ECHO ON command completed execution, DOS enabled the command-name display, displaying the VOL command.

Many users prefer to precede the commands in their AUTOEXEC.BAT file with the @ character or the ECHO OFF command. By so doing, DOS suppresses the display of command names as it executes the commands in AUTOEXEC.BAT.

ECHO Batch-File Command

Function:

Suppresses or enables the display of command names as DOS executes the command within a batch file.

Format:

ECHO ON

or

ECHO OFF

Notes:

The ECHO OFF command suppresses the display of command names within a batch file as DOS executes each command. By suppressing the display of command names, you reduce screen clutter and reduce the possibility of confusing the end user. By default, DOS uses ECHO ON, which directs DOS to display each command name as it executes. DOS will reset ECHO to ON at the end of a batch file.

If you are using DOS version 3.3 (or later) or OS/2 you can suppress command names in a batch file by preceding each name with the @ character.

In addition to enabling and disabling command-name display, the ECHO batch-file command lets your batch files display messages to the end user.

Example:

Assume that your batch file runs the DOS commands TIME and DATE, as follows:

```
TIME
DATE
```

When you run the batch file, DOS (by default) displays each command name as the command executes:

```
C> TIME
Current time is 11:26:46.03a
Enter new time:
```

(continued)

continued

```
C> DATE
Current date is Sat 05-11-1991
Enter new date (mm-dd-yy):
```

If you add the ECHO OFF and CLS commands to your batch file, as follows:

```
ECHO OFF
CLS
TIME
DATE
```

DOS suppresses the command-name display as the batch file executes, and then displays:

```
Current time is 11:26:46.03a
Enter new time:
Current date is Sat 05-11-1991
Enter new date (mm-dd-yy):
```

ENDING A BATCH FILE EARLY

If you need to end the execution of a batch file, hold down the Ctrl key and press C. When DOS detects the Ctrl-C, DOS displays the message:

```
Terminate batch job (Y/N)?
```

If you press Y, DOS immediately ends the batch-file processing. If you press N, DOS ends the command it is currently executing, continuing execution with the next command in the batch file. To better understand this processing, let's again examine the TIMEDATE.BAT batch file, which contains TIME and DATE. When you run this batch file, DOS first executes the TIME command, as follows:

```
C> TIMEDATE

Current time is 11:39:22.25a
Enter new time:
```

Rather than entering a new time, press the Ctrl-C key combination. When DOS detects the Ctrl-C, DOS asks you if you want to end the batch file, as follows:

```
C> TIMEDATE

Current time is 11:39:22.25a
Enter new time: ^C

Terminate batch job (Y/N)?
```

In this case, press Y. DOS ends the execution of the entire batch file, immediately returning control to the DOS prompt.

Run TIMEDATE.BAT a second time, and press Ctrl-C at the TIME prompt:

```
C> TIMEDATE

Current time is 11:39:22.25a
Enter new time: ^C

Terminate batch job (Y/N)?
```

This time, press N. When you press N, DOS does not end the batch file; instead, DOS ends only the current command, continuing execution with the next command in the batch file, which in this case is DATE:

```
C> TIMEDATE

Current time is 11:39:22.25a
Enter new time: ^C

Terminate batch job (Y/N)? N

Current date is Sat 05-11-1991
Enter new date (mm-dd-yy):
```

Note:

In OS/2, Ctrl-C does not offer an option. It ends the execution of the batch file, immediately returning control to the system prompt.

REDIRECTING OUTPUT WITH DOS BATCH FILES

DOS batch files I/O redirection does not work *for* batch files when you execute a batch file but will work *within* batch files. For example, if a batch file, named DIRAB.BAT, consists of:

```
DIR A:*.*
DIR B:*.*
```

and you execute that batch file by typing:

```
DIRAB > PRN
```

the DIR output will *not* be directed to the printer. To direct the DIR output to the printer, I/O redirection must be associated directly with a specific DOS command. Therefore, DIRAB.BAT would be rewritten as follows:

```
DIR A:*.* > PRN
DIR B:*.* > PRN
```

In this case, DOS will redirect the output of both DIR commands to the printer. The batch file will still display both DIR command lines on the screen as they execute. To suppress the command-name display, use the ECHO OFF command or use the @ character as follows:

```
@DIR A:*.* > PRN
@DIR B:*.* > PRN
```

HELPING OTHERS UNDERSTAND YOUR BATCH FILES

The name you give a batch file should hint at the batch file's overall purpose. As your batch files increase in complexity, however, you might have difficulty remembering not only the batch file's sequence of commands but also the switches each command line contains. To help you remember, or to help another user who is reading the file understand what the batch file does, DOS provides the batch-file command REM. REM (for Remark) allows you to place a line in your batch file that provides information to a user reading the batch file. When DOS encounters

REM, it continues execution with the next command in the batch file.

Consider how the REM command improves the readability of the batch file GETINV.BAT:

```
ECHO OFF
REM   Name: GETINV.BAT
REM   Function: Executes the commands for
REM   inventory processing.
REM
REM   Written By: K. Jamsa 6/01/91
REM
REM   Use the program CALCINV to determine
REM   the current inventory status.
CALCINV
REM   Use the program SORTINV to generate
REM   a sorted listing of the current inventory.
SORTINV
REM   Use the program PRINTINV to print
REM   hard copies of the current inventory.
PRINTINV
REM   Use the program ORDERINV to
REM   initiate inventory purchase orders.
ORDERINV
```

At first glance, the length of the batch file might be intimidating. However, after you read the remarks the operation of the batch file should become clear.

The ECHO OFF command disables the display of DOS command names as the batch file executes. If you don't include the ECHO OFF command, DOS will display each REM command on the screen as the batch file executes. (Remember: REM is meant to aid you as you read a batch file. If DOS displays each REM command on the screen as the batch file executes, your batch file will confuse the user.)

Next, lines 2 through 6 explain the purpose of the batch file, who wrote it, and when it was written. By including this information, you have a point of contact for the batch file as well as a creation date that lets you know whether or not you are using the most recent version of the batch file.

Should someone decide to change the batch file, the person changing the batch file should include a line that states the date of the change and the reason for the change.

```
ECHO OFF
REM  Name: GETINV.BAT
REM  Function:  Executes the commands for
REM  inventory processing.
REM
REM  Written by: K. Jamsa 6/01/91
REM  Last change: D. Jamsa 9/12/91 Print two
REM  inventory copies
REM
```

Even the simplest batch file can become confusing several weeks after you create it. To reduce the potential for confusion, use REM extensively in your batch files. The few minutes you spend documenting your batch file today will save you much time and effort should you later need to change the batch file.

REM Batch-File Command

Function:

Provides remarks in a batch file that explain the operation of the batch file.

Format:

REM text

Notes:

As a batch file's complexity increases, so too does the difficulty of understanding the batch file's processing. The REM batch-file command lets you place reminders in a batch file that explain its purpose. When DOS encounters a REM statement, DOS ignores it, continuing execution of the batch file with the next command in the batch file.

The ECHO OFF command suppresses the display of remarks in your batch file.

(continued)

continued

> **Example:**
>
> Your batch files should at least contain several lines at the
> top that explain who wrote the batch file and when it was
> written:
>
> ```
> REM Monthly backup procedures.
> REM Written by: K. Jamsa
> REM              06/01/1991
> REM Function: Performs a complete disk backup of
> REM           all of the files on your disk.
> ```

IMPROVING BATCH-FILE READABILITY

The REM batch-file command lets you place meaningful remarks in a batch file that you can later refer back to in order
to better understand the batch file's processing. As the number of REM statements in your batch file increases, so too
does the possibility of clutter, which leads to reader confusion.

To reduce clutter, many users place blank lines within their
batch files to separate logically related commands. By separating commands in this way, you can draw the reader's attention to specific sections of the batch file. A batch file
with small sections is less intimidating to the reader. In addition, the blank lines improve the visual appeal of the
batch file:

```
ECHO OFF
REM  Name: GETINV.BAT
REM  Function: Executes the commands for
REM  inventory processing.
REM
REM  Written by: K. Jamsa 6/01/91
REM


REM  Use the program CALCINV to determine
REM  the current inventory status.
CALCINV
```

```
REM  Use the program SORTINV to generate
REM  a sorted listing of the current inventory.
SORTINV

REM  Use the program PRINTINV to print
REM  hard copies of the current inventory.
PRINTINV

REM  Use the program ORDERINV to
REM  initiate inventory purchase orders.
ORDERINV
```

TEMPORARILY SUSPENDING BATCH-FILE PROCESSING

Many batch files execute all the commands—from the first to the last—without user intervention. For those times, however, when a batch file needs to wait until the user places a printer on line or inserts a specific floppy disk in a drive, the batch-file command PAUSE lets a batch file display a message, suspending batch-file processing until the user presses any key to continue.

When a batch file executes the PAUSE command, PAUSE displays the message specified in its command line, followed by the line:

```
Press any key to continue . . .
```

When the user presses any key, the batch file resumes processing at the next command. If, for some reason, the user wants to end the batch file's processing, the user can press the Ctrl-C key combination at the PAUSE prompt.

Consider a batch file, named PRINTDIR.BAT, that prints the files in the current directory. Before printing the directory listing, the batch file displays:

```
PAUSE Place the printer on line
Press any key to continue . . .
```

As you might have guessed, the batch file contains the following two commands:

```
PAUSE Place the printer on line
DIR > PRN
```

When you execute this batch file, PAUSE will wait for you
to press any key to continue.

The next batch file, named PAUSETWO.BAT, uses the
PAUSE command twice to obtain a printed listing of the
files in drive A. The first PAUSE tells the user to place a
disk in drive A. The second PAUSE tells the user to place
the printer on line.

```
PAUSE Put disk with directory to print in drive A
PAUSE Place the printer on line
DIR A:> PRN
```

When you run this batch file, DOS executes the first
PAUSE command and displays the following:

```
PAUSE Put disk with directory to print in drive A
Press any key to continue . . .
```

When you place a disk in drive A and press a key, the
batch file executes the second PAUSE command and displays the following:

```
PAUSE Place the printer on line
Press any key to continue . . .
```

When you place the printer on line and press a key, the
batch file executes the DIR command, redirecting the
directory output to the printer as desired.

Notice that neither of the preceding two batch files used
the ECHO OFF command to suppress the display of the
batch-file command name. As it turns out, when a batch
file sets ECHO OFF, DOS suppresses the user message
contained in the PAUSE command line. As a result, the
only output that appears on the screen is the message:

```
Press any key to continue . . .
```

The following batch file, named NOMSG.BAT, illustrates
that ECHO OFF suppresses the display of the user message
in the PAUSE command line:

```
ECHO OFF
PAUSE Place the printer on line
DIR > PRN
```

When you run this batch file, DOS displays:

```
C> ECHO OFF
Press any key to continue . . .
```

As you can see, DOS has indeed suppressed the message *Place the printer on line*.

A batch file that uses the PAUSE command is very likely to use the ECHO ON command to enable the display of some batch-file command names and the ECHO OFF command to disable others.

Consider a batch file, named ECHOTEST.BAT, that enables and disables command-name display so that the PAUSE message is not suppressed:

```
ECHO OFF
VER
VOL
ECHO ON
PAUSE Just turned ECHO ON
ECHO OFF
VER
VOL
```

When you run this batch file, DOS displays:

```
C> ECHO OFF

MS-DOS version 5.00

 Volume in drive C is DOS 5
 Volume Serial Number is 3921-18D3

C> PAUSE Just turned ECHO ON
Press any key to continue . . .

C> ECHO OFF

MS-DOS version 5.00

 Volume in drive C is DOS 5
 Volume Serial Number is 3921-18D3

C>
```

Remember: If you are using DOS version 3.3 (or later) or OS/2, you can suppress the ECHO OFF message by making the @ character the first character on the command line.

Depending on the number of commands in a batch file and on the run time of each batch file, the user is very likely to start the batch file, leave it running unattended, and move on to other tasks away from the computer. If the batch file executes a PAUSE command, a considerable amount of time might pass before the user remembers to press a key to continue batch-file processing.

Rather than using PAUSE to simply display a message to the user, you might want PAUSE to also send the bell sound to your computer's built-in speaker. As you will see, by knowing a few secrets about the ASCII character set that the computer uses to display letters, numbers, and symbols on your screen, generating the computer's bell sound becomes easy.

Each letter and number that the computer displays or that your printer prints is represented by a unique value from 0 through 127. The ASCII character set comprises these values. In addition to the uppercase and lowercase letters of the alphabet, the ASCII character set contains values for common punctuation symbols as well as special values that have unique meaning to the computer. The ASCII value 7, for example, directs the computer to send the bell sound to its built-in speaker.

For the PAUSE command to sound your computer's bell, the message in the PAUSE command line must contain ASCII 7. Several methods exist for placing this character in the PAUSE command line.

Let's begin by creating a batch file, named BELL.BAT, by copying the file from the keyboard, as follows:

```
C> COPY CON BELL.BAT
```

Type the word *PAUSE* followed by a space, but do not press Enter. Next, let's place three ASCII 7 characters in the PAUSE command line so that your computer will sound its bell three times when you execute the batch file.

Three methods are available for entering an ASCII 7 to sound the bell. The first method is to hold down the Alternate (Alt) key and press the number 7 key on your numeric keypad at the far right of your keyboard. (Note: You must use the numeric keypad—not the row of number keys across the top of your keyboard.)

Figure 4. *The numeric keypad (shaded) as it appears on the 83-key keyboard.*

When you release the Alt key, DOS writes the characters ^G (pronounced Control G) to your screen, as follows:

```
C> COPY CON BELL.BAT
PAUSE ^G
```

Press the Alt-7 key combination two more times. (Note: The Alt key must be released between successive entries of ASCII values.)

```
C> COPY CON BELL.BAT
PAUSE ^G^G^G
```

Next, complete the batch file by entering the message *BELL BELL BELL*, as follows:

```
C> COPY CON BELL.BAT
PAUSE ^G^G^GBELL BELL BELL
^Z
     1 File(s) copied

C>
```

When you run the batch file, DOS sounds your computer's bell three times, displays the message *BELL BELL BELL* followed by *Press any key to continue . . .*, and awaits your response.

DOS and OS/2 represent the ASCII 7 character on your screen with ^G. The second method of creating a batch file that sounds your computer's bell uses the Ctrl-G key combination.

As before, create the batch file BELL.BAT by copying it from the keyboard. In this case, we will simply overwrite the previous version of the file on disk. Type the word *PAUSE*, followed by a space:

```
C> COPY CON BELL.BAT
PAUSE
```

Next, hold down the Ctrl key and press the G key. DOS displays:

```
C> COPY CON BELL.BAT
PAUSE ^G
```

Repeat this process twice and then type the word *BELL* three times, creating the batch file, as follows:

```
C> COPY CON BELL.BAT
PAUSE ^G^G^GBELL BELL BELL
^Z
     1 File(s) copied

C>
```

When you run this batch file, DOS sounds your computer's bell three times, displays the words *BELL BELL BELL* on your screen, displays the message *Press any key to continue . . .*, and awaits your response.

Next, delete the file BELL.BAT so that you can create it using the DOS command EDLIN:

```
C> DEL BELL.BAT
```

The third method for sounding the bell uses Edlin to edit the file BELL.BAT:

```
C> EDLIN BELL.BAT
New file
*
```

Press the Edlin insert command, I, to enter the first line of the file. Type the word *PAUSE*, followed by a space:

```
C> EDLIN BELL.BAT

New file
*I
        1:* PAUSE
```

Press Ctrl-G three times to place the ASCII 7 character in the file, and type BELL three times:

```
C> EDLIN BELL.BAT
New file
*I
        1:* PAUSE ^G^G^GBELL BELL BELL
        2:*
```

Press Ctrl-C to exit the Edlin insert mode, and press the Edlin end command, E, to save the file's contents:

```
C> EDLIN BELL.BAT
New file
*I
        1:* PAUSE ^G^G^GBELL BELL BELL
        2:* ^C

*E

C>
```

Finally, if you are creating your batch files with a word processor, refer to the documentation that accompanied your word processor to learn how to enter an ASCII character sequence. (Later in this reference, we will use a set of values from 128 through 255, called the ASCII extended character set, that allows the IBM PC and PC compatibles to display boxes and mathematical characters.)

PAUSE Batch-File Command

Function:

Temporarily suspends the processing of a batch file after displaying an optional message to the user. When the user presses any key, the batch-file processing continues.

(continued)

continued

Format:

PAUSE [message]

Notes:

When your batch file executes PAUSE, DOS displays the optional message that appears in the PAUSE command line, followed by the message:

```
Press any key to continue . . .
```

If the user presses any key, the batch-file processing continues with the next command in the batch file. If the user does not want to continue the batch-file processing, the user can end the batch file by pressing Ctrl-C and then pressing Y to respond to the message *Terminate batch job (Y/N)?*

The ECHO OFF batch-file command suppresses the display of the optional message contained in the PAUSE command line. If your batch file specifies ECHO OFF, the PAUSE command still displays the message *Press any key to continue . . .*, and PAUSE suspends the batch-file processing until the user presses a key.

Example:

The batch file prompts the user to insert the floppy disk containing payroll information into drive A. After the user does so, the user presses any key to continue:

```
PAUSE Insert diskette PAYROLL into drive A
PAYROLL
```

When you run this batch file, DOS displays:

```
C> PAUSE Insert diskette PAYROLL into drive A
Press any key to continue . . .
```

DISPLAYING MESSAGES TO THE USER WITH THE *ECHO* BATCH-FILE COMMAND

The PAUSE batch command allows a batch file to display a message to the user. However, after each message that

PAUSE writes to the screen, the user must press a key to continue. In many cases, you will want your batch files to display messages or prompts to the user that don't require the user to continually press Enter. In such instances, the ECHO batch-file command provides a solution. In addition to letting a batch file enable and disable command-name display, ECHO lets batch files display a single-line message to the user. To use ECHO to display messages, most batch files first suppress command-name display using the ECHO OFF command. A batch file, named MESSAGE.BAT, displays the following messages:

```
First Message
Second Message
Last Message
```

This batch file's commands are:

```
ECHO OFF
CLS
ECHO First Message
ECHO Second Message
ECHO Third Message
```

The batch file first disables the command-name display by using ECHO OFF. If you remove the ECHO OFF command, the batch-file output becomes cluttered:

```
C> ECHO First Message
First Message

C> ECHO Second Message
Second Message

C> ECHO Third Message
Third Message
```

The ECHO batch command's capability to display messages has many uses, ranging from displaying batch-file menus to setting screen colors to redefining keys on your keyboard (the latter two using the ANSI.SYS device driver).

Notice how the ECHO batch command displays copyright
information in the following batch file:

```
ECHO OFF
REM  Name: GETINV.BAT
REM  Function: Executes the commands for
REM  inventory processing.
REM
REM  Written by: K. Jamsa 6/01/91
REM
REM  Display copyright information.
ECHO GETINV.BAT (Copyright 1991. KAJ Software)
ECHO All rights reserved.

REM  Use the program CALCINV to determine
REM  the current inventory status.
CALCINV

REM  Use the program SORTINV to generate
REM  a sorted listing of the current inventory.
SORTINV

REM  Use the program PRINTINV to print
REM  hard copies of the current inventory.
PRINTINV

REM  Use the program ORDERINV to
REM  initiate inventory purchase orders.
ORDERINV
```

When the user runs this batch file, DOS displays:

```
ECHO OFF
GETINV.BAT (Copyright 1991. KAJ Software)
All rights reserved.
```

As you can see, ECHO allows you to display meaningful
messages to the user without interrupting the batch file's
processing.

Many users encounter difficulty when trying to display
blank lines from a batch file using the ECHO command.
By default, if you execute ECHO with no command-line
parameter (such as the word ON or OFF, or a message),
ECHO displays its current status, ECHO ON or

ECHO OFF. For example, from the DOS prompt, call the
ECHO command:

```
C> ECHO
ECHO is on

C>
```

When you don't specify an ECHO command-line parameter, ECHO simply displays its current state. A batch file,
named SHOWECHO.BAT, calls ECHO to display its current state throughout the batch file's processing:

```
@ECHO Displaying default state
@ECHO
@ECHO Turning ECHO OFF
@ECHO OFF
@ECHO
```

When you run this batch file, DOS displays:

```
C> SHOWECHO
Displaying default state
ECHO is on
Turning ECHO OFF
ECHO is off
```

Even if you place several space characters after the ECHO
batch command, ECHO still displays its current state.
DOS 5 and OS/2 1.2 allow you to display a blank line if
you enter the ECHO command with a period immediately
following the command (ECHO.). For prior releases, the se-
cret to displaying a blank line using ECHO lies in the
ASCII extended character value 255. Your computer associates unique characters and symbols with the ASCII values 0 through 127 as well as with the ASCII extended
values 128 through 255. The ASCII character set uses the
value 32 for the blank character. If the ECHO command
line contains only blanks, ECHO displays its state. As it
turns out, the ASCII extended character value 255 also corresponds to a blank character. The ECHO command, however, does not recognize this value as a blank. Therefore, if
you place the ASCII extended character value 255 in the
ECHO command line, ECHO displays your blank line as
you intended.

Create the batch file BLANK.BAT by copying the commands from the keyboard:

```
C> COPY CON BLANK.BAT
```

The batch file begins by setting ECHO OFF and clearing the screen display:

```
ECHO OFF
CLS
ECHO Skip one line
```

To skip a line, type the word *ECHO*, followed by a space. Next, hold down the Alt key while typing *255* (using the numeric keypad). When you release the Alt key, you will see the cursor move one character position to the right. The ECHO command line now contains the ASCII extended value 255.

Use the same procedure to complete the batch file:

```
C> COPY CON BLANK.BAT
ECHO OFF
CLS
ECHO Skip one line
ECHO <Alt 255 here>
ECHO Skip two lines
ECHO <Alt 255 here>
ECHO <Alt 255 here>
ECHO Last line
^Z
        1 File(s) copied

C>
```

When you run this batch file, DOS displays:

```
Skip one line

Skip two lines


Last line
```

If ECHO displays its current state when this batch file runs, you have not correctly entered the Alt-255 key combination for the three ECHO commands that do not show any associated values. (Remember: You must use the numeric keypad.)

To create a batch file that displays a blank line using Edlin, use this same technique. After you edit the file and enter the ECHO batch command, hold down the Alt key and type *255* (using the numeric keypad):

```
C> EDLIN BLANK.BAT
New file
*I
        1:* ECHO <Alt 255 here>
```

If you are using DOS 5, you can direct ECHO to display a blank line simply by specifying ECHO. as the command line. For example, the following batch file BLANK5.BAT directs ECHO to display blank lines using the period:

```
@ECHO OFF
ECHO Skip one line
ECHO.
ECHO Skip two lines
ECHO.
ECHO.
ECHO Last line
```

As you can see, under DOS 5, displaying a blank line with ECHO. becomes easier than having to use Alt+255.

Note:

As we increase the capabilities of the batch files throughout the remainder of this quick reference, the ECHO command will prove to be one of the most valuable batch-file commands.

ECHO Message Batch-File Command

Function:

Displays a single-line message to the end user.

Format:

ECHO message

(continued)

continued

Notes:

In addition to enabling and disabling command-name display within your batch files, the ECHO batch command also lets your batch files display single-line messages to the end user. The message can be as simple as a single-line error message that tells the user a file was not found, or it can contain ANSI escape sequences that clear the screen display and set screen colors. Throughout this reference, you will use ECHO to draw menus, sound your computer's bell, and even redefine keys on your keyboard.

If you are using DOS 5, you can direct ECHO to display a blank line by specifying ECHO. as the command line.

```
ECHO.
```

If you are not using DOS 5, you can direct ECHO to display a blank line by echoing the extended ASCII character created by the Alt+255 keyboard combination.

Example:

This batch file uses ECHO to sound the computer's bell, telling the user that the inventory processing is finished:

```
ECHO OFF
CALCINV
SORTINV
PRINTINV
ORDERINV
ECHO ^G^G^GInventory processing complete
ECHO Inventory status information is printing
```

Remember: Pressing Ctrl-G results in ^G being displayed.

When this batch file completes execution, your computer's bell sounds three times, and DOS displays:

```
Inventory processing complete
Inventory status information is printing
```

WHERE TO PLACE YOUR BATCH FILES ON DISK

As you begin to create more batch files, the batch files might eventually spread out across your disk. Many users initially place their batch files in the same directory in which their DOS commands reside. After all, that directory is normally defined in the PATH= environment entry.

A better solution is to create a unique directory for those batch files that you use frequently. You can name this directory either BATCH or UTIL (for utilities):

```
C> MKDIR \BATCH
```

After you copy your batch files to this directory, you can modify the PATH statement to add the directory to your command-file search path. If you add the directory to your command path, keep in mind that DOS might have to examine each filename in the directory when it searches for your batch file. If the directory contains several seldom-used batch files, DOS is wasting time examining those filenames. Because of this, restrict the directory to your frequently used batch files.

PART IV

Using Parameters to Increase Batch-File Flexibility

GETTING STARTED WITH BATCH-FILE PARAMETERS

Batch files exist to save you time and keystrokes. Let's look at a batch file, named P.BAT, that prints a copy of the file AUTOEXEC.BAT. The batch file is very short, containing only the following command:

```
PRINT \AUTOEXEC.BAT
```

In this case, each time you want to print the contents of your AUTOEXEC.BAT file, you need only press P and then press Enter. Although P.BAT saves you a considerable number of keystrokes, it isn't very functional. You would only use it to print the contents of one specific file. A more flexible batch file would allow you to abbreviate a command such as PRINT, enabling you to use the batch file to print the contents of *any* file.

Each time you type a command at the DOS prompt, the line on which you type is the command line. DOS command lines often consist of two parts, a command name such as DISKCOPY and command-line parameters such as the disk-drive identifiers A: and B:

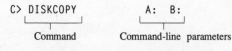

```
C> DISKCOPY          A:  B:
```
        Command   Command-line parameters

DOS provides support for batch-file parameters. Using these parameters, you can quickly create the batch file P.BAT, which abbreviates the PRINT command for any file. In this case, the batch file becomes:

```
PRINT %1
```

As you can see, the batch file contains the DOS command PRINT, as before; however, the command directs DOS to print *%1* (rather than a filename). Each time you run a batch file, DOS assigns the first command-line parameter to the symbol %1. In this case, if you run P.BAT as:

```
C> P \AUTOEXEC.BAT
```

DOS assigns to %1 the value \ AUTOEXEC.BAT, as follows:

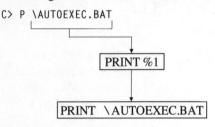

```
C> P \AUTOEXEC.BAT
```

If you later run the batch file as:

```
C> P \CONFIG.SYS
```

DOS assigns to %1 the filename \CONFIG.SYS, as follows:

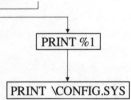

```
C> P \CONFIG.SYS
```

Because the DOS command PRINT supports wildcard characters, you can run the batch file as:

```
C> P *.BAT
```

In this case, DOS prints all the files in the current directory that have the BAT extension.

Here we have greatly increased the flexibility of the batch file by using one batch parameter. To enhance your processing capabilities to an even greater extent, DOS supports batch-file parameters %0 through %9. As you just learned, DOS assigns the first batch-file command-line parameter to the variable %1. If your batch-file command line contains several batch parameters, such as:

```
C> PAYROLL JUNE JULY AUGUST
```

DOS assigns the parameters to variables, starting with %1 and continuing through %9 (if that many exist). Each time you run a batch file, DOS assigns the name of the batch file to the variable %0. In this case, the assignments become:

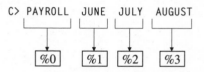

A batch file, named SHOWNAME.BAT, uses the ECHO batch-file command to display its own name:

```
ECHO OFF
CLS
ECHO %0
```

When you run this batch file, DOS displays:

```
SHOWNAME
```

By using the ECHO batch command, you can display the values of the batch-file parameters %0 through %9. Although this is seldom necessary, should your batch file ever need to use its own name during its processing, DOS provides the name using %0.

A batch file, named SHOWVAR.BAT, uses the ECHO batch-file command to display each of the parameters %0 through %9:

```
ECHO OFF
CLS
ECHO %0 %1 %2 %3 %4 %5 %6 %7 %8 %9
```

If you run the batch file with the command line:

```
C> SHOWVAR ONE TWO THREE
```

DOS displays:

```
C> SHOWVAR ONE TWO THREE
SHOWVAR ONE TWO THREE
```

Likewise, if you run the batch file with:

```
C> SHOWVAR A B C D E F G H
```

DOS displays:

```
C> SHOWVAR A B C D E F G H
SHOWVAR A B C D E F G H
```

Batch-file parameters are essential to powerful batch files. A batch file, named CP.BAT, uses the batch-file parameters %1 and %2 to abbreviate the COPY command:

```
COPY %1 %2
```

If you run this batch file as:

```
C> CP \AUTOEXEC.BAT \AUTOEXEC.SAV
```

DOS assigns the parameters, as follows:

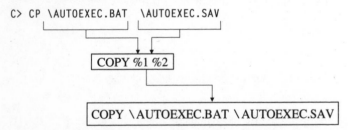

Later in this reference you will learn how to use the batch-file commands IF and FOR. As you will see, DOS batch parameters greatly increase batch-file functionality.

PART V

Batch-File Programming

TESTING SPECIFIC CONDITIONS WITHIN YOUR BATCH FILES

All the batch files we have examined so far have started with the first command in the batch file, executing the commands from top to bottom. As your batch files increase in complexity, you might want or need to control which batch commands DOS will execute, based on a specific set of conditions. The IF batch-file command gives a batch file the capability to execute a DOS command only when a given condition is true.

The IF batch command allows a batch file to test six unique conditions: The three IF conditions—EXIST, StringOne==StringTwo, and ERRORLEVEL—can be complemented by a NOT condition, yielding six conditions.

The first condition is whether a specific file exists on disk. To use the IF command to determine whether a file exists, your command format becomes:

```
IF EXIST filename.ext  DOSCommand
```

When DOS encounters the IF command, DOS examines the disk for the specified file. The filename parameter can contain a complete DOS pathname, beginning with a disk-drive letter and a complete string of subdirectory names, or it can simply be a filename that DOS searches for in the current directory. In either case, if the file exists, DOS executes the specified command. If the file does not exist, DOS continues with the next command in the batch file.

The second IF batch condition allows you to specify:

```
IF NOT EXIST filename.ext DOSCommand
```

The effect of this command format is that if the specified file does *not* exist, the specified command is executed.

If you create a batch file, named T.BAT, that uses the batch parameter %1 to abbreviate the DOS command TYPE, as follows:

```
TYPE %1
```

and then run this batch file with a filename that does not exist, DOS displays the message:

```
File not found — filename.ext
```

This batch file is very well suited for the IF EXIST batch-file command. The batch file can first test to see if the specified file exists on disk. If the file exists, the batch file executes the TYPE command. If the file does not exist, DOS does not execute the TYPE command, so no error messages occur. The new T.BAT file contains:

```
IF EXIST %1 TYPE %1
```

Experiment with this batch file by running it with existing files as well as with files that do not exist.

As you know, the DOS command COPY overwrites an existing file on disk if the file is not a read-only, system, or hidden file. To prevent an errant COPY command from overwriting a critical file, you might want to create a simple batch file, named MYCOPY.BAT, that uses the IF EXIST batch-file command to determine whether the target file already exists. If the target file exists on disk, the batch file can use the PAUSE batch-file command to warn the user. The user can then press any key to continue the file copy operation. (Note: The result of the file copy operation will be the message *Access denied - filename.ext* if the target file has one or more of the read-only, system, or hidden attributes; in none of these three cases will the target file be overwritten.) Alternatively, the user can press Ctrl-C to terminate the batch file. For example, if the batch file MYCOPY.BAT contains:

```
IF EXIST %2 PAUSE Target file already exists
COPY %1 %2
```

and if the target file exists on disk, the batch file displays:

```
C> IF EXIST FILENAME.EXT PAUSE Target file
                            already exists
Press any key to continue . . .
```

The user can cancel the command by pressing Ctrl-C. (Note: Due to width constraints, the *C>* command line shown above runs over to the next line.)

You might even want to take the processing one step further by including the %2 batch parameter in the message that PAUSE displays, as follows:

```
IF EXIST %2 PAUSE Target file %2 already exists
COPY %1 %2
```

In this case, if the user runs the batch file with AUTOEXEC.BAT as the target file, the batch file displays:

```
C> IF EXIST AUTOEXEC.BAT PAUSE Target file
                AUTOEXEC.BAT already exists
Press any key to continue . . .
```

The user now knows immediately why the batch file is displaying the PAUSE message. (Note: Due to width constraints, the *C>* command line shown above runs over to the next line.)

IF EXIST Batch-File Command

Function:

Tests whether a file exists and, if so, executes the specified DOS command.

Format:

IF EXIST filename.ext DOSCommand

Notes:

The IF EXIST condition searches the disk for the specified file. The filename can be a complete DOS pathname that starts with a disk-drive letter and a directory name, or it can be a filename that DOS searches for in the current directory.

(continued)

continued

> If DOS locates the specified file, DOS executes the speci-
> fied command. If the file does not exist, DOS continues
> batch-file execution with the next command in the
> batch file.
>
> **Example:**
> This batch file tests whether the file AUTOEXEC.BAT ex-
> ists in the root directory. If the file exists, the batch file
> prints a copy of it and then proceeds to the VER command.
> If the file does not exist, DOS continues batch-file execu-
> tion with the VER command:
>
> ```
> IF EXIST \AUTOEXEC.BAT PRINT \AUTOEXEC.BAT
> VER
> ```

The third IF batch condition tests whether two character
strings are equal. A character string is a sequence of one or
more characters. The format of this IF condition is:

IF StringOne==StringTwo DOSCommand

If the character strings on both sides of the double equal
sign are the same, DOS executes the specified command. If
the strings differ, DOS continues execution with the next
command in the batch file.

The fourth IF batch condition tests to determine if two
character strings are *not* equal. The format becomes:

IF NOT StringOne==StringTwo DOSCommand

If DOS finds that the two strings differ, the specified command is executed. If the two strings are equal, DOS continues execution with the next batch-file command.

A batch file, named COLOR.BAT, examines the color
name specified by the first batch parameter, %1:

```
ECHO OFF
IF %1==RED ECHO Color is Red
IF %1==BLUE ECHO Color is Blue
IF %1==WHITE ECHO Color is White
```

Run the batch file as:

C> `COLOR BLUE`

and the batch file displays:

`Color is Blue`

Next, run the batch file with the color *RED*:

C> `COLOR RED`

DOS matches the expression:

`IF %1==RED ECHO Color is Red`

As a result, DOS displays:

`Color is Red`

For the IF batch command to consider two strings as the same, the strings must match letter for letter, including use of uppercase and lowercase. If you run the batch file with the color *Blue*:

C> `COLOR Blue`

DOS does not find a matching color, because the IF batch command does not recognize the strings *Blue* and *BLUE* as the same.

A good way to better understand the processing that the IF batch command performs is to remove the ECHO OFF command from the previous batch file. If you then run the batch file as:

C> `COLOR BLUE`

you can see the actual comparisons that the DOS batch file performs.

Next, try running the batch file without a command-line parameter, such as:

C> `COLOR`

Each time DOS attempts to execute an IF command, it displays the message:

`Syntax error`

DOS displays this message because the syntax or format of the IF command is invalid. Remember: The IF batch command compares two strings. If you do not assign a value to the batch parameter %1, the IF command has only one string to compare. Because DOS requires two strings, DOS displays a syntax-error message. To prevent this problem, you need to ensure that the IF command always has two strings to compare. To do so, you group the strings within quotes:

```
IF  "%1"=="RED" ECHO Color is Red
IF  "%1"=="BLUE" ECHO Color is Blue
IF  "%1"=="WHITE" ECHO Color is White
```

In this case, if the user enters the command:

C> COLOR BLUE

the batch file matches the condition:

```
IF "BLUE"=="BLUE" ECHO Color is Blue
```

If the user does not enter a color, the comparison becomes:

```
IF ""=="RED" ECHO Color is Red
```

The quotes are called the *empty string*. Because the IF command can compare the empty string with the color values, we eliminate the syntax error.

A batch file, named TEST%1.BAT, uses the empty string to test the value of %1. If you don't specify a batch parameter, the batch file displays the following message:

No parameter value specified

In many batch files, you will need to test whether the user has specified a value for %1:

IF "%1"=="" ECHO No parameter value specified

If the user runs the batch file simply as:

C> TEST%1

the IF condition becomes:

```
IF ""=="" ECHO No parameter value specified
```

IF StringOne==StringTwo Batch-File Command

Function:

Tests if two character strings are identical, and if so, executes the DOS command that follows.

Format:

IF StringOne==StringTwo DOSCommand

Notes:

The IF StringOne==StringTwo condition compares two character strings letter by letter. If the strings match exactly, including use of uppercase and lowercase, DOS executes the command that follows. If one or more letters differ, DOS continues the batch-file processing with the next command in the batch file.

If you do not specify two character strings in the IF batch command line, DOS displays the following error message:

```
Syntax error
```

This error is common when you are testing a batch parameter that does not have a value, such as:

```
IF %1==MONTHLY_BACKUP GOTO MONTHLY
```

In this case, if the user does not specify a value for %1, the IF condition becomes:

```
IF==MONTHLY_BACKUP GOTO MONTHLY
```

Because the command contains only one string, DOS displays the *Syntax error* message. As a solution, simply place the character strings to be compared within quotes, as follows:

```
IF "%1"=="MONTHLY_BACKUP" GOTO MONTHLY
```

In this case, if the user does not specify a value for %1, DOS will compare the empty string with the string MONTHLY_BACKUP, as follows:

```
IF ""=="MONTHLY_BACKUP" GOTO MONTHLY
```

(continued)

continued

Because the command line contains two strings, DOS does not generate the *Syntax error* message.

Example:

This batch file tests whether the value of the batch parameter is \AUTOEXEC.BAT. If it is, the batch file prints \AUTOEXEC.BAT:

```
IF "%1"=="\AUTOEXEC.BAT" PRINT \AUTOEXEC.BAT
```

The next batch file uses the IF command to determine which language the user would like to use:

```
IF "%1"=="GERMAN" GOTO GERMAN
IF "%1"=="SPANISH" GOTO SPANISH
IF "%1"=="FRENCH" GOTO FRENCH
IF "%1"=="SWEDISH" GOTO SWEDISH
GOTO INVALID_LANGUAGE
```

This batch file simply compares the value of %1 with the specified languages. If %1 matches one of the languages, the batch file branches to the corresponding label. If %1 does not match a language, the batch file branches to the label INVALID_LANGUAGE.

The fifth IF batch condition tests the exit or ending status of the previous DOS command. As it turns out, many of the DOS commands return a status value that indicates whether or not they successfully completed execution—and if not, why not. For example, the DOS command DISKCOPY returns one of the following exit-status values:

Value	Error Status
0	Disk copy successful
1	Copy unsuccessful, nonfatal disk error
2	Copy incomplete, user Ctrl-C
3	Copy unsuccessful, fatal disk error
4	Insufficient memory or invalid drive

The IF ERRORLEVEL batch-file command lets your
batch files examine a command's exit-status value and
continue processing accordingly. The format of the
IF ERRORLEVEL batch command is:

IF ERRORLEVEL value DOSCommand

When DOS encounters the IF ERRORLEVEL command,
DOS examines the exit-status value of the previous command. If the exit status is greater than or equal to the specified status value, DOS executes the specified command. If
the exit-status value is less than the specified value, DOS
continues processing with the next command in the batch
file. The sixth condition tests to determine whether the
EXIT status is *not* equal to or greater than the specified
value. If the EXIT status is *less than* the specified value,
the specified DOS command is executed; otherwise, processing continues with the next batch-file command.

A batch file, named ERRLEVEL.BAT, tests to see if the
user has terminated the DOS command DISKCOPY with
the Ctrl-C key combination. If the user has terminated the
DISKCOPY command by pressing Ctrl-C, DISKCOPY returns an exit-status value of 2.

```
@DISKCOPY A: B:
@IF ERRORLEVEL 2 ECHO Ctrl-C Termination
```

Run the batch file ERRLEVEL.BAT:

```
C> ERRLEVEL
```

When DISKCOPY displays the prompt:

```
Insert SOURCE diskette in drive A:

Insert TARGET diskette in drive B:

Press any key to continue . . .
```

press Ctrl-C to terminate the command. When you do so,
DOS displays:

```
Ctrl-C Termination
```

When DOS continues the batch file's execution at the IF
command, DOS compares DISKCOPY's exit-status value

with the value 2. In this case, because the values are equal, the batch file displays the message:

```
Ctrl-C Termination
```

Keep in mind that as long as the previous command's exit-status value is greater than or equal to the specified value, DOS executes the command associated with the IF batch command. (Note: If DISKCOPY had terminated because of *fatal disk error* or *insufficient memory or invalid drive* [exit-status values 3 and 4, respectively], the condition would also be true, and the specified DOS command would be executed.)

The ability to test and utilize exit-status values will be key to increasing the functionality of the batch files that appear later in this reference. Your goal in creating a batch file is to automate a series of DOS commands. With that in mind, your batch files should be able to handle unexpected errors. The IF ERRORLEVEL batch command lets your batch files do exactly that.

IF ERRORLEVEL Batch-File Command

Function:

Tests the exit-status value of the previous program. If the program's exit-status value is greater than or equal to the value given, execute the specified DOS command.

Notes:

Many programs return an exit-status value to DOS that indicates whether they successfully completed execution. For example, the DOS command FORMAT returns the following exit-status values:

```
Value        Meaning
0            Successful format
3            Format incomplete due to user Ctrl-C
4            Format incomplete due to an error
5            User termination at the prompt:

             WARNING, ALL DATA ON NON-REMOVABLE DISK
             DRIVE x: WILL BE LOST!
             Proceed with Format(Y/N)?
```

(continued)

continued

The IF ERRORLEVEL batch-file command lets your batch files test a program's exit-status value and then continue processing accordingly.

Not all DOS commands provide exit-status values.

When DOS encounters an IF ERRORLEVEL batch-file command, DOS compares the exit status of the previous DOS command with the value the IF batch command specifies. If the exit status is greater than or equal to the value in the IF command, DOS executes the corresponding command. If the exit-status value is less than the specified value, the batch-file processing continues with the next command in the batch file. (This logic is reversed if the *IF NOT ERRORLEVEL* expression—the sixth condition— is used.)

Example:

This batch file executes the DOS command FORMAT and displays a completion status message based on FORMAT's exit-status value:

```
ECHO OFF
FORMAT A:
IF ERRORLEVEL 5 GOTO NO_RESPONSE
IF ERRORLEVEL 4 GOTO ERROR
IF ERRORLEVEL 3 GOTO USER_CTRLC
ECHO Successful FORMAT operation
GOTO DONE
:NO_RESPONSE
ECHO Fixed disk will not be formatted
GOTO DONE
:ERROR
ECHO Error in processing, FORMAT incomplete
GOTO DONE
:USER_CTRLC
ECHO FORMAT incomplete due to Ctrl-C
:DONE
```

(continued)

continued

Notice that the batch file tests the highest exit-status value first.

Remember: If the exit-status value is greater than or equal to the value in the IF batch-file command, DOS executes the specified command. If this batch file first tested for an exit status of 3, DOS would always perform the processing for *user Ctrl-C*, regardless of whether the exit status was 3, 4, or 5. In all three error cases, the exit status would be greater than or equal to 3. By reversing the order of the tests, the batch file branches to the correct position for each status value.

USING THE *NOT* OPERATOR

As you just learned, the IF batch-file command lets your batch files execute a DOS command when a specific condition is met. The condition can be the existence of a specific file, two strings being identical, or a command's exit-status value being greater than or equal to the specified value. In many batch-file applications, it is more convenient for DOS to perform a specific command when a tested condition *fails*. The batch-file command NOT operator allows you to do exactly that.

The NOT operator changes the result of a condition. If, for example, a condition evaluates as true, using the NOT operator returns a false result. Likewise, if the result of an expression is false, the NOT operator returns a true value.

Consider this change to the batch file T.BAT. The batch file begins by testing whether the file specified by %1 exists on disk. If so, the batch file displays the file's contents. Next, the batch file performs a second test. This test allows the batch file to display the message:

```
filename.ext does not exist
```

The batch file T.BAT now becomes:

```
ECHO OFF
CLS
IF EXIST %1 TYPE %1
IF NOT EXIST %1 ECHO %1 does not exist
```

In this case, if the result of the EXIST %1 condition is false (meaning the file does not exist), the NOT operator changes the result to true and directs IF to execute the ECHO command. If instead, the result of the condition is true (the file exists), the NOT operator changes the result to false. When the IF batch command examines the false value, it does not execute the ECHO command.

The NOT operator is used extensively in DOS batch files. A batch file, named COMPSTR.BAT, compares the two strings contained in the batch parameters %1 and %2. If the strings are identical, the batch file displays the message:

string1 and *string2* are identical

If the strings differ, the batch file displays the message:

string1 and *string2* are not the same

This batch file's commands are:

```
ECHO OFF
CLS
IF "%1"=="%2" ECHO %1 and %2 are identical
IF NOT "%1"=="%2" ECHO %1 and %2 are not the same
```

As you can see, the batch file needs two IF batch commands to perform its processing. The first IF command handles the condition where the strings are the same. The second IF command handles the condition where the strings differ. (For programmers, this processing might seem similar to that of an IF-ELSE statement.)

NOT Batch-File Operator

Function:

Reverses a true or false result in an IF batch-file command. If the result of a test is false, NOT changes the result to true. Likewise, if the result of a test is true, NOT changes the result to false.

Format:

IF NOT condition DOSCommand

Notes:

The NOT operator can be used with any one of the three IF conditions:

```
IF NOT EXIST filename.ext DOSCommand
IF NOT StringOne == StringTwo DOSCommand
IF NOT ERRORLEVEL value DOSCommand
```

Example:

This batch file tests whether the \AUTOEXEC.BAT batch file exists in the root directory on the current drive. If not, the batch file displays messages that tell the user to create the file.

```
ECHO OFF
IF NOT EXIST \AUTOEXEC.BAT GOTO NO_FILE
GOTO DONE
:NO_FILE
ECHO Your root directory does not contain the batch
ECHO file AUTOEXEC.BAT. This batch file lets you
ECHO specify one or more commands that you want DOS
ECHO to execute each time your system starts. Most
ECHO users place the DOS PRINT, PROMPT, and PATH
ECHO commands in this file.
:DONE
```

(continued)

continued

Assuming that the batch file AUTOEXEC.BAT does not reside in the root directory of the default drive, the batch file displays:

```
Your root directory does not contain the batch
file AUTOEXEC.BAT. This batch file lets you
specify one or more commands that you want DOS
to execute each time your system starts. Most
users place the DOS PRINT, PROMPT, and PATH
commands in this file.
```

REPEATING A DOS COMMAND FOR A SET OF FILES

As you just found, the IF batch-file command lets your batch files perform a DOS command when a specific condition is met. Processing that is dependent on whether a specific condition is true or false is called *conditional processing*. In addition to conditional processing within your batch files using IF, DOS lets you repeat a specific command for a specific set of files. Processing that executes at least one time, possibly repeating, is called *iterative processing*. The batch-file command FOR lets your batch files repeat a command for a specific set of files.

The format of the FOR batch command is:

FOR %%BatchVar IN (SetOfFiles) DO DOSCommand

Like all commands specific to batch-file processing, FOR is an internal command. DOS always keeps internal commands in memory (as opposed to external commands, such as DISKCOPY, that reside on disk).

The second entry in the FOR command, *%%BatchVar*, is a batch variable. Earlier we discussed the batch variables %0 through %9 that DOS substitutes values for during the batch file's processing. The variable *%%BatchVar* is similar in that DOS again assigns a value to this variable. The difference is simply in naming. Most batch files use the letters of the alphabet to name batch variables, such as %%A or %%F. DOS restricts the names of batch variables to one letter. The word IN is part of the FOR command. IN tells DOS that the set of files FOR is to use follows immediately (between the left and right parentheses).

The FOR batch command executes by assigning each filename in a given set of files to the batch variable. After DOS has assigned the first filename, DOS executes the DOS command that follows. When the command completes execution, DOS assigns the next filename in the set to the batch variable and this process repeats. When no files remain in the set, the FOR batch command completes execution.

You specify the set of files by simply typing filenames, separated by either a space or a comma. The following sets of files are examples of valid sets for the FOR batch command:

(MAY.PAY JUNE.PAY JULY.PAY)

(MAY.PAY, JUNE.PAY, JULY.PAY)

(*.BAT *.EXE *.COM)

(*.*)

As you can see, FOR supports the DOS wildcard character * (asterisk), as seen in the above example, as well as the ? (question mark). When FOR detects a wildcard, DOS expands the wildcard into the corresponding set of filenames. FOR, in turn, uses the filenames one at a time.

The word DO tells DOS that the command to execute for each file immediately follows. The DOS command can be any DOS command. To better understand this processing, consider the command:

FOR %%A IN (A.BAT B.BAT C.BAT) DO TYPE %%A

Here, FOR first assigns the file A.BAT to the variable %%A, and DOS then executes the command TYPE %%A. Because DOS has assigned the filename A.BAT to the batch variable, DOS actually executes the command TYPE A.BAT.

When the TYPE command completes execution, FOR assigns the next file in the set to the batch variable. In this

case, DOS displays the contents of the file B.BAT. Again,
when the TYPE command completes execution, FOR repeats this process, assigning the filename C.BAT to the
variable.

When the TYPE command completes execution, FOR
again examines its set of files. Because no more files remain, the FOR command completes execution.

In a similar manner, the next batch file, named
SHOW.BAT, uses the FOR batch command to display all
the batch files in the current directory:

```
FOR %%I IN (*.BAT) DO TYPE %%I
```

The FOR command uses the variable %%I. The actual variable name you use does not matter. You must, however,
use a single-letter name, as previously discussed.

By default, the DOS command DIR displays a file's name,
extension, size, and creation date and time:

```
COMMAND   COM     46246 12-13-90   4:09a
COMP      EXE     13930 12-13-90   4:09a
COUNTRY   SYS     13496 12-13-90   4:09a
DEBUG     EXE     20506 12-13-90   4:09a
DISKCOMP  COM     10428 12-13-90   4:09a
DISKCOPY  COM     11393 12-13-90   4:09a
DISPLAY   SYS     15682 12-13-90   4:09a

     .       .         .    .          .
     .       .         .    .          .
     .       .         .    .          .

XCOPY     EXE     15624 12-13-90   4:09a
```

If you call DIR with the /W qualifier, DIR displays only
filenames and extensions. However, DIR displays five
filenames across the screen. In some cases, you might simply want to display filenames one after another, as follows:

```
COMMAND.COM
COMP.EXE
COUNTRY.SYS
DEBUG.EXE
DISKCOMP.COM
DISKCOPY.COM
DISPLAY.SYS

   .
   .
   .

XCOPY.EXE
```

The next batch file, named SHORTDIR.BAT, uses the FOR batch command to echo filenames (with ECHO) to the screen, as follows:

```
ECHO OFF
CLS
FOR %%I IN (*.*) DO ECHO %%I
```

Here, the FOR batch-file command assigns the name of each file in the current directory to the variable %%I. DOS then uses the ECHO command to display the filename on the screen. As discussed, if your FOR command contains wildcard characters, DOS expands the wildcard characters into the corresponding filenames.

By using batch-file parameters, we can increase the flexibility of SHORTDIR.BAT. In this case, rather than displaying the names of each file in the current directory by using the asterisk wildcard characters (*.*), the batch file now lets you specify the desired wildcard filename as the first command-line parameter. For example:

```
C> SHORTDIR *.BAT
```

or:

```
C> SHORTDIR *.TXT
```

To display all of the files in the current directory, your command line becomes:

```
C> SHORTDIR *.*
```

To provide this flexibility, simply change SHORTDIR.BAT to read:

```
ECHO OFF
CLS
FOR %%I IN (%1) DO ECHO %%I
```

A batch file, named SORTDIR.BAT, is for advanced DOS users. It uses the DOS redirection operations to display a sorted directory listing of the files specified by the first command-line parameter.

```
@ECHO OFF
IF EXIST SORTFILE.DAT DEL SORTFILE.DAT
FOR %%I IN (%1) DO ECHO %%I >> SORTFILE.DAT
```

```
SORT < SORTFILE.DAT
DEL SORTFILE.DAT
```

This batch file first uses the IF EXIST condition to delete the file SORTFILE.DAT if the file exists. Next, the FOR batch command "echoes" (with ECHO) each filename (as the previous batch file did). In this case, however, the batch file uses the redirection operator to direct the output of the ECHO command from the screen, appending the output to the file SORTFILE.DAT. After FOR has created the file of filenames, the batch file uses the DOS command SORT to sort the file's contents, displaying the sorted filenames on the screen display. When the SORT command completes execution, it deletes the file SORTFILE.DAT, cleaning up after itself because the file is no longer needed.

Using the FOR batch command, you can improve the batch file T.BAT so that it supports the DOS wildcard characters:

```
ECHO OFF
CLS
FOR %%I IN (%1) DO TYPE %%I
```

In so doing, the command:

```
C> T *.BAT
```

displays the contents of all of the batch files that reside in the current directory. In fact, you might want to include several of the batch parameters in FOR's set of files, as follows:

```
ECHO OFF
CLS
FOR %%I IN (%1 %2 %3 %4 %5) DO TYPE %%I
```

After you do this, your batch-file command line can specify several files to display:

```
C> T SORTDIR.BAT SHORTDIR.BAT *.BAT
```

Now the batch file displays the contents of SORTDIR.BAT, followed by those of SHORTDIR.BAT. Next, the batch file expands the wildcard characters *.BAT and displays all the files in the current directory on the default drive with the extension BAT.

FOR Batch-File Command

Function:

Repeats a DOS command for a given set of files.

Format:

FOR %%v IN (set) DO DOSCommand

Notes:

When you run the FOR batch-file command, FOR assigns the first file specified in the set of files to the specified variable. The variable must have a single-letter name. You specify the set of files by typing filenames separated by either a comma or a space. After the FOR batch command assigns a filename to the specified variable, FOR issues the specified DOS command. When the DOS command completes execution, FOR assigns the next file in the set of files to the variable, and this process repeats.

When no more files remain in the set of files, the FOR command completes execution, and the batch file continues processing with the next command in the batch file.

Example:

The FOR command fully supports the DOS wildcard characters. If the set of files contains wildcard characters, FOR expands each wildcard into the appropriate list of filenames, assigning each to the variable, one at a time.

This batch file uses the FOR command to issue the DOS command TYPE and displays the contents of the files A.TXT, B.TXT, and C.TXT:

```
FOR %%I IN (A.TXT B.TXT C.TXT) DO TYPE %%I
```

In a similar manner, the following batch file uses the type command to display the contents of all the files associated with the %1 parameter. If the user runs the batch file with a wildcard character, such as the asterisk in *.BAT, the batch file displays the contents of each corresponding file:

```
FOR %%V IN (%1) DO TYPE %%V
```

The FOR batch command adds tremendous flexibility to batch files, and it will be used repeatedly throughout the remainder of this reference.

BRANCHING FROM ONE POSITION IN A BATCH FILE TO ANOTHER WITH *GOTO*

All the batch files we have examined throughout this reference have started with the first command in the batch file, executing commands one after another from top to bottom. When we examined the IF batch-file command, you learned that you can direct DOS to execute a command only when a specific condition is met. As your applications increase in complexity, you might occasionally need the batch file to perform a specific set of commands in one instance or to skip one or more commands in another. The GOTO batch-file command lets your batch file branch from one command to another. The format of the GOTO batch command is:

GOTO DOSBatchLabel

Let's take a look at a simple example. A batch file, named REMOVE.BAT, uses the batch parameter %1 to display a file's contents. After the batch file displays the file's contents, it displays the message:

```
PAUSE About to delete filename.ext
Press any key to continue . . .
```

If the user presses a key, the batch file deletes the file. If the user does not want to delete the named file, the user ends the batch file by pressing the Ctrl-C key combination.

```
ECHO OFF
IF "%1"=="" GOTO NO_FILE
TYPE %1
PAUSE About to delete %1
DEL %1
GOTO DONE
:NO_FILE
ECHO Need to specify filename
:DONE
```

REMOVE.BAT begins by testing whether the user has specified a file as a command-line parameter. If not, the batch file branches to the label NO_FILE, as follows:

```
ECHO OFF
IF "%1"=="" GOTO NO_FILE
TYPE %1
PAUSE About to delete %1
DEL %1
GOTO DONE
:NO_FILE
ECHO Need to specify filename
:DONE
```

In this case, DOS displays the message:

```
Need to specify filename
```

and ends. As you can see, the GOTO batch command branches control to the specified label. A batch label begins with a colon and can contain any number of characters—although DOS recognizes only the first eight. This batch file uses the labels :NO_FILE and :DONE. Notice that the line containing the label begins with a colon and that the label reference in the GOTO command does not:

```
ECHO OFF
IF "%1"=="" GOTO NO_FILE          ———— Label references in
TYPE %1                                 GOTO commands
ECHO About to delete %1
PAUSE
DEL %1
GOTO DONE
:NO_FILE
ECHO Need to specify filename    ———— DOS labels with colons
:DONE
```

When DOS encounters a line in your batch file that begins with a colon, DOS knows the line contains a label. In such a case, DOS does not attempt to execute the label as a command. Also, regardless of the state of ECHO, labels are not displayed when a batch file is run.

In the batch file REMOVE.BAT, if the user presses a key to delete the file, the batch file issues the command DEL and then uses GOTO to branch to the label :DONE at the end of the batch file.

As you will learn, applications for batch files are basically limitless. For example, the batch file HELPDOS.BAT provides a general on-line help facility for DOS. To get help on a specific DOS command, the user runs the batch file with a specified command. For example:

C> `HELPDOS FORMAT`

The batch file in turn examines the first batch parameter (%1) and displays the corresponding help text:

```
FORMAT command

Command type: External

Function: Prepares a disk for use by DOS.

Command format: FORMAT [drive:][/B][/1][/4][/8]
[/N:sectors] [/S][/T:tracks][/V:disklabel][/F:size]
[/U | /Q]

Example: FORMAT A:/4
```

The batch file is quite simple to create. To begin, the batch file tests to ensure that the user has provided a batch parameter. If not, the batch file uses the GOTO batch command to branch to commands that instruct the user on how to use the batch file:

```
ECHO OFF
IF "%1"=="" GOTO INSTRUCTIONS
```

Next, assuming that the user has provided a batch parameter, the batch file tests one DOS command after another to determine the DOS command with which the user wants help:

```
IF "%1"=="CLS" GOTO CLS_HELP
IF "%1"=="FORMAT" GOTO FORMAT_HELP
IF "%1"=="DISKCOPY" GOTO DISKCOPY_HELP
       .
       .
       .
IF "%1"=="XCOPY" GOTO XCOPY_HELP
```

As you can see, depending on the value of %1, the batch file branches to a specific position within the batch file. In the case of the CLS command, for example, the batch file contains:

```
:CLS_HELP
ECHO CLS command
ECHO <Alt-255>*
ECHO Command type: Internal
ECHO <Alt-255>*
ECHO Function: Erases the screen display,
ECHO placing the cursor at the upper left,
ECHO or home, position
ECHO <Alt-255>*
ECHO Example: CLS
GOTO DONE
```

*To enter ASCII 255, you must hold down the Alt key and type *255* using the numeric keypad. Remember, with DOS 5, you can generate a blank line on the screen by typing *ECHO.* instead.

If the user runs the batch file with:

```
C> HELPDOS CLS
```

the batch file displays:

```
CLS command

Command type: Internal

Function: Erases the screen display,
placing the cursor at the upper left,
or home, position

Example: CLS
```

After the batch file displays the help information on a specific topic, the batch file uses the GOTO batch command to branch to the ending label :DONE.

As you can guess, a complete batch-file command help facility for all the DOS commands could get quite large. Instead, the following version of HELPDOS.BAT provides on-line help for the batch-file commands IF, FOR, and GOTO:

```
ECHO OFF
IF "%1"=="" GOTO INSTRUCTIONS
IF "%1"=="IF" GOTO IF_HELP
IF "%1"=="FOR" GOTO FOR_HELP
```

```
IF "%1"=="GOTO" GOTO GOTO_HELP
ECHO Invalid command
:INSTRUCTIONS
ECHO The batch file provides on-line help for
ECHO IF, FOR, and GOTO. Run the batch file
ECHO as HELPDOS command name, such as
ECHO HELPDOS GOTO
GOTO DONE
:IF_HELP
ECHO IF Command
ECHO <ALT-255>•
ECHO Command type: Internal, batch
ECHO <ALT-255>•
ECHO Function: Allows a batch file to perform
ECHO           decision making using one of the
ECHO           following conditions:
ECHO               IF EXIST filename.ext DOSCommand
ECHO               IF ERRORLEVEL value DOSCommand
ECHO               IF StringOne==StringTwo DOSCommand
ECHO <Alt-255>•
ECHO Example: IF EXIST %1 PRINT %1
GOTO DONE
:FOR_HELP
ECHO FOR Command
ECHO <Alt-255>•
ECHO Command type: Internal, batch
ECHO <Alt-255>•
ECHO Function: Repeats a DOS command for a set
ECHO           of files.
ECHO <Alt-255>•
ECHO Format: FOR %%Var IN (set) DO DOSCommand
ECHO <Alt-255>•
ECHO Example: FOR %%I IN (*.*) DO TYPE %%I
GOTO DONE
:GOTO_HELP
ECHO GOTO Command
ECHO <Alt-255>•
ECHO Command type: Internal, batch
ECHO <Alt-255>•
ECHO Function: Lets a batch file branch from one
ECHO           location to another.
ECHO <Alt-255>•
ECHO Format: GOTO label
ECHO <ALT-255>•
```

```
ECHO Example: :Repeat
ECHO          VER
ECHO          GOTO REPEAT
:DONE
```

* To enter ASCII 255, you must hold down the Alt key and type *255* using the numeric keypad. Remember, with DOS 5, you can generate a blank line on the screen by typing *ECHO*. instead.

PART VI

Advanced Batch-File Concepts

USING NAMED PARAMETERS

As you have seen, the DOS batch parameters %0 through %9 increase your batch file's capabilities, allowing a single batch file to serve several applications. In addition to these batch parameters, DOS versions 3.3 and later support *named parameters*. A named parameter is a batch variable enclosed in percent signs. When DOS encounters a named parameter in your batch file, DOS searches the DOS environment for a corresponding entry. For example, a batch file, named PRT.BAT, prints the file that corresponds to the named parameter %PRINT_FILE%:

```
PRINT %PRINT_FILE%
```

When DOS encounters %PRINT_FILE% in your batch file, DOS searches the DOS environment for an entry in the form:

```
PRINT_FILE=
```

The DOS command SET allows you to change or display entries in the DOS environment. If you issue the SET command without a command line, as follows:

```
C> SET
```

DOS displays the current environment entries:

```
COMSPEC=C:\DOS\COMMAND.COM
PATH=C:\DOS
```

To create an environment entry, issue the SET command and assign a value to the environment entry, as follows:

```
C> SET PRINT_FILE=AUTOEXEC.BAT
```

If you issue the SET command again, DOS displays its
new entry:

```
C> SET
COMSPEC=C:\DOS\COMMAND.COM
PATH=C:\DOS
PRINT_FILE=AUTOEXEC.BAT
```

If you run the batch file PRT.BAT, DOS replaces the named
parameter PRINT_FILE with the corresponding environment
entry AUTOEXEC.BAT, printing the file's contents.

To remove an environment entry, use the SET command,
as follows:

```
C> SET PRINT_FILE=
```

In this case, DOS removes the PRINT_FILE entry, leaving
the contents of the environment as:

```
C> SET
COMSPEC=C:\DOS\COMMAND.COM
PATH=C:\DOS
```

If you again run the batch file PRT.BAT, DOS will not
find an environment entry that matches PRINT_FILE;
therefore, the named parameter will contain the empty
string. Using the IF batch-file command, the batch file can
test for the empty string and continue processing accordingly, as follows:

```
ECHO OFF
IF "%PRINT_FILE%"=="" GOTO NO_PARAMETER
PRINT %PRINT_FILE%
GOTO DONE
:NO_PARAMETER
ECHO The named parameter PRINT_FILE is
ECHO not defined. Use the DOS SET command
ECHO to assign it the filename to print.
:DONE
```

Many users have trouble thinking of applications that need
named parameters, so let's look at one or two examples.
First, consider a batch file that might create temporary files
as it executes. Some users might not want DOS to create
the files in the current directory. Consider the following

batch file, which creates the temporary file
SORTDIR.TMP:

```
DIR | SORT > SORTDIR.TMP
PRINT SORTDIR.TMP
MORE < SORTDIR.TMP
DEL SORTDIR.TMP
```

If the user starts this batch file and then later ends it using
the Ctrl-C key combination before the DEL command completes execution, the file SORTDIR.TMP remains in the
current directory. As an alternative, a user might want to
create a directory, named TEMPDIR, that stores the temporary files. Next, a user would place references to the directory TEMPDIR throughout the batch file, as follows:

```
DIR | SORT > \TEMPDIR\SORTDIR.TMP
PRINT \TEMPDIR\SORTDIR.TMP
MORE < \TEMPDIR\SORTDIR.TMP
DEL \TEMPDIR\SORTDIR.TMP
```

The problem with this method is that it forces all users to
create a TEMPDIR directory to hold the temporary files.

The following batch file, named NAMEDTMP.BAT, uses
a named parameter to solve the problem of where to place
temporary files:

```
DIR | SORT > %TEMPDIR%SORTDIR.TMP
PRINT %TEMPDIR%SORTDIR.TMP
MORE < %TEMPDIR%SORTDIR.TMP
DEL %TEMPDIR%SORTDIR.TMP
```

When DOS encounters the named parameter
%TEMPDIR%, DOS searches the environment for a
corresponding entry. If no such entry exists, DOS assigns
%TEMPDIR% to the empty string. As such, DOS creates
the file SORTDIR.TMP in the current directory. If the user
instead creates an environment entry, such as:

```
C> SET TEMPDIR=D:
```

DOS uses the named parameter to create the file
D:SORTDIR.TMP. This batch file solves the needs of both
users. Users who don't care if DOS creates the file in the
current directory simply run the batch file without issuing

a SET command to define TEMPDIR. Users who want DOS to create the file in a specific directory, such as in a fast RAM disk, simply use SET to equate an appropriate disk, subdirectory, or both to the named parameter.

As discussed, the PATH= entry defines the list of sub-directories that DOS searches for external commands. Most users define PATH= using the PATH command in AUTOEXEC.BAT. When you install various third-party software packages, the installation often includes the newly created directory in the command path. To do so, the installation changes the contents of the batch file AUTOEXEC.BAT.

Assume, for this example, that the file AUTOEXEC.BAT contains the following commands:

```
ECHO OFF
PRINT /D:LPT1 /Q:32
PATH C:\DOS
```

Next, assume that a software installation wants to add the directory C:\UTIL to the command path. Rather than changing the entry:

```
PATH C:\DOS
```

the installation can add the line:

```
SET PATH=%PATH%;C:\UTIL
```

at the end of the batch file. The entry takes advantage of the fact that the DOS command PATH creates a DOS environment entry. After the PATH entry exists, you can use it as a named parameter.

To better understand how this processing works, create a batch file, named MYPATH.BAT, that contains:

```
ECHO OFF
SET MYPATH=C:\DOS
ECHO Appending C:\UTIL to %MYPATH%
SET MYPATH=%MYPATH%;C:\UTIL
ECHO Complete entry is %MYPATH%
```

When you run this batch file, DOS displays:

```
Appending C:\UTIL to C:\DOS
Complete entry is C:\DOS;C:\UTIL
```

As you can see, the batch file created the complete entry, C:\DOS;C:\UTIL, as intended.

Several of the batch files that we will examine throughout the remainder of this reference will use DOS named parameters.

RUNNING ONE BATCH FILE FROM WITHIN ANOTHER

All the commands executed by our batch files so far have been either EXE or COM files. If your batch file needs to run another batch file, your batch file needs to use either the DOS command COMMAND or the DOS command CALL, depending on your version of DOS.

To understand why your batch file cannot execute a second batch file simply by calling the name of the batch file as you would a DOS command, let's create a simple batch file, named VERVOL.BAT, that contains:

```
VER
VOL
```

Next, create a batch file, named PRIMARY.BAT, that contains:

```
DATE
VERVOL
TIME
```

PRIMARY.BAT runs the batch file VERVOL.BAT by referencing the batch file's name. When you run the batch file PRIMARY.BAT, DOS first executes the DATE command and displays the following:

```
C> PRIMARY
C> DATE
Current date is Sat 05-11-1991
Enter new date (mm-dd-yy):
```

If you press Enter (leaving the date unchanged), DOS runs the second batch file, VERVOL.BAT. As DOS executes this batch file, DOS displays:

```
C> PRIMARY
C> DATE
Current date is Sat 05-11-1991
Enter new date (mm-dd-yy):

C> VERVOL

C> VER

MS-DOS version 5.00

C> VOL

 Volume in drive C is DOS 5
 Volume Serial Number is 3921-18D3

C>
```

The batch file VERVOL.BAT completed execution, but DOS did not execute the TIME command that is the last command in the batch file PRIMARY.BAT. This occurred because you must use one of the DOS commands—COMMAND or CALL—to run a second batch file, or DOS will quit executing batch-file commands when the last batch file completes execution and attempts to return to the batch file that ran it.

If you are using DOS version 3.3 or later, the CALL command lets a batch file correctly execute the commands in a second batch file and then return to the next command in the first batch file. The format of the DOS command CALL is:

CALL BatchFile [parameters]

The parameters are the optional batch parameters that DOS assigns to the variables %1 through %9. If you are using DOS version 3.3 or later, change the batch file PRIMARY.BAT to:

```
DATE
CALL VERVOL
TIME
```

When you run this batch file, DOS again executes the DATE command. As before, press Enter (leaving the system date unchanged). DOS now executes the DOS command CALL, which in turn executes the batch file VERVOL.BAT.

When VERVOL.BAT completes execution, DOS continues execution of the commands in PRIMARY.BAT, executing the TIME command. As a result, DOS displays:

```
C> PRIMARY
C> DATE
Current date is Sat 05-11-1991
Enter new date (mm-dd-yy):

C> CALL VERVOL

C> VER

MS-DOS version 5.00

C> VOL

 Volume in drive C is DOS 5
 Volume Serial Number is 3921-18D3

C> TIME
Current time is  1:54:09.09p
Enter new time:

C>
```

CALL Batch-File Command

Function:

Allows one batch file to run another batch file, followed by a return to the initial batch file.

Format:

CALL BatchFile [parameters]

(continued)

continued

Notes:

If you run one batch file from within another without using
CALL or COMMAND /C (discussed in the second para-
graph following this summary box), DOS will only execute
commands until one batch file completes execution. If you
run a second batch file from the middle of a batch file, the
commands in the first batch file that follow the command
which invokes the second batch file will never execute.
When the second batch file ends, the execution of all batch
commands ends.

If you are using DOS version 3.3 or later, the CALL batch-
file command lets you run one batch file from within another, followed by a return to the initial batch file. Simply
place the name of the batch file on the CALL command
line, along with any batch parameters.

Example:

This batch file uses the CALL batch command to run the
batch file NESTED.BAT:

```
VER
CALL NESTED
VOL
```

In this case, NESTED.BAT contains:

```
DATE
TIME
```

If you remove the CALL command from the first batch
file, leaving:

```
VER
NESTED
VOL
```

DOS will never execute the VOL command. When
NESTED.BAT completes execution, DOS stops executing
batch-file commands and returns to the system prompt.

As you can see, the CALL command allows a batch file
to successfully run a second batch file and to return to
the first file for executing the remaining commands.

If you are using a DOS version earlier than 3.3, you
must use COMMAND /C to run a second batch file. The
file COMMAND.COM contains the DOS command-line
processor. The command-line processor executes
commands as you type them at the DOS prompt, as well
as the commands in a DOS batch file. If you are using a
DOS version earlier than 3.3, change the batch file
PRIMARY.BAT so that it contains:

```
DATE
COMMAND /C VERVOL
TIME
```

Be sure that the file COMMAND.COM resides in the current directory or in the command path.

```
C> DIR COMMAND.COM
 Volume in drive C is DOS 3.1
 Directory of  C:\DOS

COMMAND  COM    23210 03-07-85  1:43p
        1 File(s)   21104640 bytes free

C>
```

When you run the batch file, DOS executes the DATE
command. As before, press Enter to leave the system date
unchanged. The batch file's processing will continue,
using COMMAND /C to run the batch file VERVOL.BAT.
When VERVOL.BAT completes execution, DOS continues with the execution of the TIME command in the batch
file PRIMARY.BAT. DOS then displays:

```
C> PRIMARY
C> DATE
Current date is Sat 05-11-1991
Enter new date (mm-dd-yy):

C> COMMAND /C VERVOL

C> VER

IBM DOS Version 3.10
```

```
C> VOL

 Volume in drive C is DOS 3.1

C> TIME
Current time is  13:54:09.09
Enter new time:

C>
```

COMMAND /C directs DOS to load a second command
processor in memory. The /C tells DOS that the command
processor will remain in memory only to execute the command that follows. In this case, the secondary command
processor remains in memory just long enough to execute
the commands in the batch file VERVOL.BAT. When the
batch file completes execution, DOS removes the secondary command processor from memory and continues execution of the commands in the initial batch file.

COMMAND /C Batch-File Command

Function:
Allows one batch file to run another batch file, followed by
a return to the initial batch file.

Format:
COMMAND /C BatchFile [parameters]

Notes:
If you run one batch file from within another without using
CALL or COMMAND /C, DOS will only execute commands until one batch file completes execution. If you run
a second batch file from the middle of a batch file, the commands in the first batch file that follow the command that
invokes the second batch file will never execute. When the
second batch file ends, the execution of all batch commands ends.

If you are using DOS version 3.2 or earlier, COMMAND
/C lets you run one batch file from within another. Simply
place the name of the batch file on the COMMAND /C
batch-file command line, along with any batch parameters.

(continued)

continued

Example:

This batch file uses COMMAND /C to run the batch file NESTED.BAT:

```
VER
COMMAND /C NESTED
VOL
```

In this case, NESTED.BAT contains:

```
DATE
TIME
```

If you remove COMMAND /C from the first batch file, leaving:

```
VER
NESTED
VOL
```

DOS will never execute the VOL command. When NESTED.BAT completes execution, DOS stops executing batch-file commands and returns to the system prompt.

As your batch files increase in complexity, you might on occasion choose to provide the user with a list of menu options. Each menu option results in the execution of a different DOS command. One of the options might allow the user to temporarily suspend the batch file's execution so that the user can execute commands from the DOS prompt. The DOS command COMMAND lets your batch files do exactly that.

Consider a batch file, named USEDOS.BAT, that contains:

```
ECHO OFF
CLS
ECHO In batch file, about to
ECHO access DOS prompt
COMMAND
ECHO Back in batch file
```

When DOS encounters COMMAND, DOS loads a secondary command processor into memory, which in turn displays a DOS prompt, allowing the user to execute DOS commands. When the user no longer wants to execute DOS commands, the user calls the DOS command EXIT to end the secondary command processor.

If the file COMMAND.COM resides in the current directory or in the command-file search path, issue the batch file USEDOS.BAT. In this case, DOS displays:

```
In batch file, about to
access DOS prompt


MICROSOFT(R) MS-DOS(R) Version 5.00

        (C)Copyright Microsoft Corp 1981-1991

C>
```

DOS has loaded a secondary command processor, allowing you to issue commands at the DOS prompt. In this case, issue the DATE command to display the current system date. To return control to the batch file, issue the EXIT command. Your screen now contains:

```
In batch file, about to
access DOS prompt

MICROSOFT(R) MS-DOS(R) Version 5.00

        (C)Copyright Microsoft Corp 1981-1991

C> DATE
Current date is Sat 05-11-1991
Enter new date (mm-dd-yy):

C> EXIT
Back in batch file
C>
```

When the EXIT command completes execution, DOS returns control to the batch file, which continues its execution.

HANDLING MORE THAN NINE PARAMETERS WITH *SHIFT*

As you have learned, the DOS batch-file parameters %1 through %9 let the user pass nine values to your batch file. When you pass values to batch files in this manner, your batch files increase in flexibility, supporting many more applications than batch files that don't support parameter processing. Even so, for some applications, the nine-parameter restriction can still cause problems. For such applications, the DOS batch-file command SHIFT provides a solution.

The primary purpose of the DOS command SHIFT is to allow batch files to access more than nine batch parameters. When your batch file executes SHIFT, DOS moves each batch parameter value one position to the left. DOS assigns to parameter %0 the value of %1. Likewise, DOS assigns to %1 the value of %2. DOS shifts the value of each parameter in this fashion. If your command line contains more than nine parameters, SHIFT assigns the tenth parameter to %9. If no additional parameter remains, SHIFT assigns the empty string to %9. As an example, let's consider a batch file, named ONESHIFT.BAT, that contains:

```
ECHO OFF
CLS
ECHO %0 %1 %2 %3 %4 %5 %6 %7 %8 %9
SHIFT
ECHO %0 %1 %2 %3 %4 %5 %6 %7 %8 %9
```

If you run this batch file by typing:

```
C> ONESHIFT A B C
```

DOS displays:

```
ONESHIFT A B C
A B C
```

If you run this batch file with more than nine parameters, as follows:

```
C> ONESHIFT 1 2 3 4 5 6 7 8 9 10 11
```

DOS displays:

```
ONESHIFT 1 2 3 4 5 6 7 8 9
1 2 3 4 5 6 7 8 9 10
```

Notice that SHIFT assigns the value 10 to the parameter %9. Pictorially, this SHIFT operation becomes:

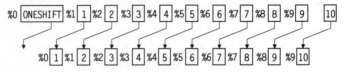

Next, a batch file, named TWOSHIFT.BAT, uses the SHIFT command twice:

```
ECHO OFF
CLS
ECHO %0 %1 %2 %3 %4 %5 %6 %7 %8 %9
SHIFT
ECHO %0 %1 %2 %3 %4 %5 %6 %7 %8 %9
SHIFT
ECHO %0 %1 %2 %3 %4 %5 %6 %7 %8 %9
```

If you run the batch file as:

```
C> TWOSHIFT A B C
```

DOS displays:

```
TWOSHIFT A B C
A B C
B C
```

As before, if you run the batch file with more than nine batch parameters, as follows:

```
C> TWOSHIFT 1 2 3 4 5 6 7 8 9 10 11
```

DOS displays:

```
TWOSHIFT 1 2 3 4 5 6 7 8 9
1 2 3 4 5 6 7 8 9 10
2 3 4 5 6 7 8 9 10 11
```

Keep in mind that when SHIFT no longer has values to assign to %9, SHIFT assigns the empty string to %9. By testing for the empty string, you can create a batch file, named SHIFTIT.BAT, that uses the GOTO command to loop through all the batch-file command-line parameters, displaying each on individual lines using ECHO:

```
ECHO OFF
:REPEAT
ECHO %0
SHIFT
IF NOT "%0"=="" GOTO REPEAT
```

If you run the batch file as:

```
C> SHIFTIT ONE TWO THREE
```

DOS displays:

```
SHIFTIT
ONE
TWO
THREE
```

When the batch file first begins execution, %0 contains the name of the batch file. When the batch file executes the SHIFT command, DOS assigns the word *ONE* to %0. Because %0 is not equal to the empty string, the batch file issues the GOTO command, and this process repeats. After the fourth SHIFT command, %0 contains the empty string, and the batch file ends.

Using this same technique, you can change the SHIFTIT.BAT batch file slightly to create a batch file, named D.BAT, to enhance the DOS command DIR:

```
ECHO OFF
CLS
:REPEAT
DIR %1
SHIFT
IF NOT "%1"=="" GOTO REPEAT
```

You can now run the batch file as:

```
C> DIR *.* *.BAT COMMAND.COM
```

The batch file in turn performs successive directory listings for the specified files. If you replace the line:

```
DIR %1
```

with:

```
FOR %%A IN (%1) DO TYPE %%A
```

the batch file uses the TYPE command to display each of the files you specify in the batch-file command line.

SHIFT Batch-File Command

Function:

Shifts each batch-file parameter value one parameter location to the left. Thus, DOS places the value of %1 in %0. Likewise, DOS assigns to %1 the value of %2, to %2 the value of %3, and so on.

Format:

SHIFT

Notes:

DOS supports the batch parameters %0 through %9. If your command line contains more than nine parameters, the SHIFT command lets your batch file access the additional parameters. Assume, for example, that a user runs a batch file, named SHIFTTST.BAT, with:

```
C> SHIFTTST A B C D
```

The batch parameter

%0 contains SHIFTTST
%1 contains A
%2 contains B
%3 contains C
%4 contains D
%5 contains "" (empty string)

If the batch file issues a SHIFT command, DOS shifts each parameter, resulting in:

%0 contains A
%1 contains B
%2 contains C
%3 contains D
%4 contains "" (empty string)
%5 contains "" (empty string)

(continued)

continued

If the command line contains more than nine parameters, SHIFT places the first unreferenced parameter into %9 with each iteration. When no additional parameters remain, SHIFT assigns %9 the empty string.

Example:

This batch file uses SHIFT to display all the batch parameters passed on the command line.

```
:Repeat
If "%1"=="" GOTO NO_MORE
ECHO %1
SHIFT
GOTO REPEAT
:NO_MORE
```

The batch file simply loops, displaying the current value of %1. As long as %1 is not the empty string, the loop continues and a new parameter value is shifted into %1.

BATCH-FILE EXCEPTIONS

You have seen each of the DOS batch-file processing commands. Now let's take a look at several problems you can encounter when you execute your batch files. If your batch file displays the message:

```
Bad command or file name
```

a command in the batch file is invalid. The quickest way to determine which command is responsible for the error message is to remove ECHO OFF so that DOS displays command names as the batch file executes. The incorrect command name will appear on your screen immediately before the error message. For example, a batch file, named BADCMD.BAT, contains an invalid DOS command:

```
VER
XYZ12345
VOL
```

When you run this batch file, DOS displays:

```
C> VER
MS-DOS version 5.00

C> XYZ12345
Bad command or file name

C> VOL

 Volume in drive C is DOS 5
 Volume Serial Number is 3921-18D3

C>
```

DOS displays the error message immediately following the command XYZ12345. When a batch file contains an invalid command, DOS displays the error message and continues execution with the next command. In many cases, a command in your batch file is a *valid* DOS command—yet DOS still issues the message *Bad command or file name* when DOS encounters the command. In such cases, the problem is not the command name but rather where DOS is searching on disk to locate the command.

Remember: DOS defines commands as either internal or external. The internal commands (such as TYPE, DATE, CLS, and VER) always reside in your computer's memory after DOS starts. External commands reside on disk. Common external commands include DISKCOPY and FORMAT. When DOS executes these commands, DOS must first find the command on disk and then load the command into memory. If the command does not reside in the current directory or in the specified directory, DOS displays the *Bad command or file name* error message simply because DOS cannot locate the file on disk. As discussed earlier in this reference, the PATH command increases the number of locations DOS searches for commands. If you know that the command generating the *Bad command* error message is valid, then be sure that DOS can locate the command.

Finally, some users have encountered the *Bad command* error message even when all the commands in their batch files can be successfully located. When this occurs, the word processor you are using has very likely embedded a strange character in the batch file that DOS cannot understand. If you are creating your batch files with a word processor, be sure you process and save the file in nondocument (ASCII) mode.

If your batch file displays the message:

```
File not found
```

the commands in your batch file are valid, but DOS cannot locate a file that one of the commands is trying to use. Consider a batch file, named BADFILE.BAT, that contains:

```
TYPE 12345678.XYZ
```

When you run this batch file, DOS displays:

```
File not found

C>
```

Although DOS successfully executed the TYPE command, TYPE could not locate the file 12345678.XYZ.

As your batch files increase in complexity, they will make extensive use of batch-file and named parameters. By using the IF EXIST condition, your batch files can test to ensure that a file exists before the batch file tries to use the file.

You will recall that the GOTO batch-file command lets your batch files branch from one location within a file to another. When DOS encounters a GOTO batch command, DOS begins searching the batch file for the specified label. If DOS encounters the label, DOS continues the batch-file execution at the command that immediately follows the label. If, instead, the label does not exist, DOS stops executing the batch file and displays the message:

```
Label not found
```

If this error occurs, be sure that your batch file contains the label and that the label is spelled correctly. The following batch file, named NOLABEL.BAT, shows that DOS immediately stops batch-file execution when a label is invalid:

```
GOTO DONE
VER
VOL
```

When you execute this batch file, DOS displays:

```
Label not found
```

Notice that DOS did not execute either the VER or the VOL command.

Also, keep in mind that DOS uses only the first eight letters of a label's name. If DOS cannot distinguish between two labels, DOS uses the first label it encounters. A batch file, named 2LABELS.BAT, uses the labels *BatchLabelOne* and *BatchLabelTwo*. Because the first eight letters of each label's name are the same, DOS views the labels as identical:

```
:BatchLabelOne
VER
GOTO BatchLabelTwo
VOL
:BatchLabelTwo
```

When you run this batch file, DOS repeatedly displays the current version number until you use the Ctrl-C key combination to end the command. Although the GOTO command references the label *BatchLabelTwo*, DOS uses only the first eight characters of the label name. Therefore, DOS repeatedly loops back to the start of the batch file.

COMPLETING THE OS/2 BATCH-FILE COMMANDS

OS/2 executes all the batch-file commands we have examined in this reference. In addition to these commands, OS/2 provides three others: EXTPROC, SETLOCAL, and ENDLOCAL.

The OS/2 EXTPROC command lets your batch file define a command processor other than the OS/2 command-line interpreter to execute the commands your batch file contains. Most users will not use EXTPROC. The format of the EXTPROC command is:

EXTPROC [drive:][path]filename.ext [arguments]

The filename provides the complete DOS path to the file, including the filename extension, to serve as the

batch file's command interpreter. Typically, you would
purchase such a file from a third-party software company.
The arguments are optional command-line arguments that
the command interpreter uses to get started. These parameters will depend entirely on the command processor you
are using.

Because EXTPROC tells OS/2 the name of the batch-file
command-line interpreter, EXTPROC must be the first
command in your batch file.

As you have found, batch files let you change the default
drive and directory, as well as the environment entries. In
some cases, you might want these changes to exist only
during execution of the batch file. For example, consider a
batch file, named CHANGEIT.BAT, that sets the environment entry FILE to FILENAME.EXT, sets the current
directory on the default drive to the root, and sets the
default drive to drive A:

```
SET FILE=FILENAME.EXT
CHDIR \
A:
```

OS/2 EXTPROC Batch-File Command

Function:
Defines the command-line processor that the batch file will
use to issue its commands.

Format:
EXTPROC [drive:][path]filename.ext [parameters]

Notes:
Most users will never use EXTPROC. The EXTPROC
batch-file command lets you use a third-party software
package to execute the commands in a batch file.

Because EXTPROC defines the command-line processor
that the batch file is to use, EXTPROC must be the first
command in the batch file.

When you run this batch file, all the changes remain in effect after the batch file completes execution. Consider, instead, an application that issues these three commands as part of its overall processing. When the batch file completes execution, the current drive and directory should be the same as when the user started the batch file. Likewise, the environment should contain its original contents.

The OS/2 SETLOCAL and ENDLOCAL batch-file commands work together to save and later restore the OS/2 environment, as well as the current disk drive and directory.

By using the SETLOCAL batch command, changes to the environment and to the current drive or directory last only as long as the batch file executes. Use of the ENDLOCAL batch command allows these values to be reset, earlier, within the batch file.

Consider a batch file, named NOCHANGE.BAT, that uses SETLOCAL and ENDLOCAL:

```
SETLOCAL
SET FILE=NEWNAME.EXT
CHDIR \
A:
ENDLOCAL
```

When OS/2 encounters the SETLOCAL batch command, OS/2 saves the current disk drive, the current directory, and the environment's contents. When OS/2 later encounters the ENDLOCAL batch command, OS/2 restores the previous settings. As a result, the batch-file changes are limited to the life of the batch file or are in effect only until an ENDLOCAL batch command is encountered.

OS/2 SETLOCAL and ENDLOCAL Batch-File Commands

Function:

Save and later restore the current disk drive, the current directory, and the contents of the OS/2 environment.

Format:

SETLOCAL
batch_commands
ENDLOCAL

Notes:

Many batch files change the contents of the environment or the current disk drive or directory during their processing.

In most cases, these changes need to be in effect only during processing of the batch file.

Unfortunately, most batch files don't restore the current disk drive or directory when they complete execution. The end user has to issue other commands to get back to the previous drive or directory.

The SETLOCAL and ENDLOCAL OS/2 batch-file commands work together to save and later restore the current drive, the current directory, and the contents of the environment. The SETLOCAL batch command saves the current values. Later, when the batch file has completed execution, the ENDLOCAL batch command restores the values. If the SETLOCAL command is used but the ENDLOCAL command is omitted, OS/2 restores the values when the batch file completes execution.

Example:

This batch file runs SETLOCAL to save the current disk drive, directory, and environment. Next, the batch file changes the current drive and directory and issues several SET commands to change environment entries. Before the batch file completes execution, it runs ENDLOCAL, which restores the saved settings. As a result, the changes

(continued)

continued

to the current disk drive, the current directory, and the environment's contents are only temporary.

```
SETLOCAL
A:
CD \
SET FILE=TEST.BAT
SET PATH=A:
SET PROMPT=A$g
ENDLOCAL
```

Part VII

Using DOSKEY and Defining DOSKEY Macros

As you have learned, DOS batch files can save time and reduce keystrokes. If you are using DOS 5, you can use the powerful DOSKEY command to simplify your work even more. After you invoke DOSKEY, DOS builds a list containing the names of each command executed from the DOS prompt. Using your keyboard arrow keys, you can quickly traverse this list, repeating or slightly modifying previously entered commands. To better understand this process, invoke DOSKEY as shown here:

C> DOSKEY

DOSKEY installed.

If DOSKEY is already installed, you will not receive the *DOSKEY installed* message, in which case you should enter DOSKEY /REINSTALL for this exercise.

Next, invoke the DOS CLS, VER, and VOL commands. As each command executes, DOS records the command's name in a list. Using your keyboard arrow keys, you can cycle through the list, recalling on the command line commands you may want to repeat:

Up Arrow	Recalls the command issued immediately before the command currently displayed.
Down Arrow	Recalls the command issued immediately after the command currently displayed.
PgUp	Recalls the oldest command in the list.
PgDn	Recalls the newest command in the list.

Experiment with your keyboard arrow keys, cycling through the commands CLS, VER, and VOL.

Each time you recall a command, DOS places the cursor at the end of the command, so you can execute the command quickly by pressing Enter. If you want to change the command before executing it, DOS lets you use the following editing keys:

Left Arrow	Moves the cursor one position to the left.
Right Arrow	Moves the cursor one position to the right.
Ctrl+Left Arrow	Moves the cursor one word to the left.
Ctrl+Right Arrow	Moves the cursor one word to the right.
Home	Moves the cursor to the start of the command.
End	Moves the cursor to the end of the command.
Esc	Clears the command from display.
Backspace	Deletes the character immediately to the left of the cursor.
Delete	Deletes the character at the cursor.

In addition, DOS lets you edit the most recent command using the standard command editing function keys, F1 through F5.

F1	Copies one character from the previous command template to the current command line.
F2	Copies the text in the previous command template up to, but not including, the first letter you type after pressing F2.
F3	Copies the remainder of the previous command template to the current command line.
F4	Deletes from the previous command template all of the characters up to and including the first letter you type after pressing F4. Note that nothing is displayed, but the new template can be displayed using F1, F2, or F3.
F5	Copies the current command line into the previous command template and clears current command line.

The DOSKEY /HISTORY switch directs DOSKEY to display the list of buffered command names. In this case, DOSKEY will display the commands CLS, VER, and VOL as shown here.

```
C> DOSKEY /HISTORY
CLS
VER
VOL
C>
```

DOSKEY defines F7 as a short-cut key for displaying the command history. When you display the commands using F7, DOSKEY precedes each command name with its relative number.

```
1: CLS
2: VER
3:>VOL
```

Note that the VOL command is preceded by the > character to indicate it is the current command. If you press the F9 function key, DOSKEY prompts you to enter the line number of the desired command:

```
C> Line number:
```

In this case, if you type 1 and press Enter, DOSKEY places CLS in the current command line. Likewise, the value 2 selects VER.

As you work with DOS throughout the day, the ability to quickly repeat previous commands using DOSKEY's command-recall capability will save you considerable time and typing.

CREATING MACROS WITH DOSKEY

In addition to letting you quickly recall previous commands, DOSKEY also lets you create RAM macros, which are similar to simple batch files. Macros, like batch files, can contain one or more commands that DOS associates with the macro name. Unlike a DOS batch file that has the BAT extension and resides on disk, macros reside in your computer's fast electronic RAM. When you turn off your computer, the macros are lost. You can place DOSKEY commands in your AUTOEXEC.BAT file to define your most commonly used macros each time your system starts.

To create a macro, you must specify the macro name and the macro's commands on DOSKEY's command line. As a result, macros are fairly short. If a macro contains more than one command, use the $T or $t metacharacter to separate them.

The following DOSKEY command creates a macro named CLSVV that clears your screen display and then executes the VER and VOL commands.

```
C> DOSKEY CLSVV=CLS $T VER $T VOL
```

You must specify the macro name (in this case, CLSVV), followed by the equal sign. Notice that the macro uses $T to separate commands. To execute this macro, simply type the macro name at the DOS prompt and press Enter.

```
C>CLSVV
```

As you have found, the batch-file parameters %1 through %9 greatly increase the capabilities of your batch files. DOSKEY macros also support command-line parameters. In the case of macros, however, you access the parameters using the symbols $1 through $9. The following macro SHOWEM uses these symbols to display its command-line parameters.

```
C> DOSKEY SHOWEM=ECHO $1 $2 $3 $4 $5 $6 $7 $8 $9
```

If you invoke SHOWEM with the letters A, B, and C, your screen displays the following:

```
C> SHOWEM A B C
C> ECHO A B C
A B C
```

DOSKEY macros don't support the SHIFT command that moves parameters one position to the left. Instead, DOSKEY macros support the $* metacharacter, which DOS replaces with the macro's command line minus the macro name. The following command creates a macro named SHOWIT that displays its command line using $*:

```
C> DOSKEY SHOWIT=ECHO $*
```

Note that, like DOS batch files, the macro displays the
name of the command as the command executes. Unlike
DOS batch files, you cannot disable the macro command
name display using ECHO OFF.

Many users create a directory using MKDIR and then immediately use CHDIR to select the directory as the current directory. The following macro MDCD creates the specified
directory and immediately selects the directory as current:

```
C> DOSKEY MDCD=MKDIR $1 $T CHDIR $1
```

To create the directory TEST and select the directory as
the current directory, you would invoke the macro as follows:

```
C> MDCD TEST
```

If you create a macro with the same name as an existing
macro, DOSKEY overwrites the existing macro in its
buffer. The following command, for example, changes the
macro SHOWEM to display each parameter on its own line.

```
C> DOSKEY SHOWEM=FOR %I IN ($*) DO ECHO %I
```

DOSKEY macros also support the DOS I/O redirection operators. To use the redirection operators, your macros must
specify the following symbols.

$G or $g	DOS output redirection operator >
$L or $l	DOS input redirection operator <
$B or $b	DOS pipe redirection operator |

The following macro, PRINTDIR, uses the redirection operators to print a sorted directory listing:

```
C> DOSKEY PRINTDIR=DIR $B SORT $G PRN
```

Admittedly, you could have used the DIR /O operator to
create the sorted directory, eliminating the need for the
SORT command. However, in this case, the macro's goal
was to illustrate the $B and $G metacharacters.

The DOSKEY /MACROS switch directs DOSKEY to
display its current list of macros. Assuming that you have

created the macros we've discussed, DOSKEY displays the following:

```
C> DOSKEY /MACROS
CLSVV=CLS $t VER $t VOL
MDCD=MKDIR $1 $t CHDIR $1
SHOWIT=ECHO $*
SHOWEM=FOR %I IN ($*) DO ECHO %I
PRINTDIR=DIR $b SORT $g PRN
C>
```

WHAT MACROS CAN'T DO

As discussed earlier, macros are similar but not identical to batch files. Macros, for instance, don't support the ECHO OFF command to disable command name display. Likewise, you cannot use the GOTO command within a macro to branch from one location to another. DOS lets you run a batch file from within a macro, but you cannot run a macro from within a batch file. You can, however, use a batch file to define one or more macros. In addition, you cannot invoke one macro from within another. Lastly, to end a macro, you must press the Ctrl-C keyboard combination for each macro command.

DOSKEY Command

Function:

Lets you recall and edit previously issued commands using your keyboard's arrow keys, and lets you define macros containing one or more DOS commands.

Format:

[drive:][path]DOSKEY [/REINSTALL]
[/BUFSIZE=BufferSize][/MACROS | /M][/HISTORY | /H]
[/INSERT | /OVERSTRIKE][MacroName=MacroText][/?]

(continued)

continued

Notes:

DOSKEY is a memory-resident software program. The /REINSTALL switch directs DOSKEY to install a new version of itself in memory, and to clear all commands and macros from the buffer.

DOSKEY stores your commands and macros in a buffer in memory. The /BUFSIZE=BufferSize switch lets you specify the size of this buffer the first time you invoke DOSKEY or use the /REINSTALL switch. The default buffer size is 1024. If you are creating a large number of macros, you may want to increase the buffer size to 4096.

The DOSKEY /MACROS switch directs DOSKEY to display the macros currently in memory. Likewise, the /HISTORY switch directs DOSKEY to display the list of the command names in the buffer.

The /INSERT switch directs DOS to behave as if the Ins key is constantly active. The /OVERSTRIKE switch disables text insert.

The /? switch displays a help panel for DOSKEY.

To create a macro, you must specify a macro name, followed by an equal sign and the macro's text (or commands). Separate commands with the $T or $t metacharacter.

Examples:

The following command directs DOSKEY to display the current command buffer and defined macros:

```
C> DOSKEY /HISTORY /MACROS
```

The following DOSKEY command creates a macro named CP that abbreviates the DOS COPY command:

```
C> DOSKEY CP=COPY $*
```

PART VIII

Getting the Most from Batch Files with ANSI.SYS and DEBUG

UNLEASHING BATCH-FILE APPLICATIONS WITH THE *ANSI.SYS* DEVICE DRIVER

If you examine your DOS disks, you will find a file with the name ANSI.SYS:

```
C> DIR ANSI.SYS

 Volume in drive C is DOS 5
 Volume Serial Number is 3A2F-18E9
 Directory of  C:\DOS

ANSI     SYS      8868 12-13-90  4:09a
         1 File(s)       8868 bytes
                     21231616 bytes free
```

The filename extension SYS tells you that ANSI.SYS is an operating-system file. Specifically, ANSI.SYS is a device driver that increases the capabilities of the computer's screen and keyboard. (A *device driver* is software that DOS loads into memory each time your system starts.) After it is installed, the device driver provides capabilities that are not available through DOS itself.

To install a device driver, you must place a DEVICE= entry in the CONFIG.SYS file. You will recall that DOS

uses CONFIG.SYS each time your system starts, to configure itself in memory. For ANSI.SYS, your CONFIG.SYS
entry becomes:

```
DEVICE=ANSI.SYS
```

You must provide DOS with a complete pathname to the
file ANSI.SYS. Therefore, if ANSI.SYS resides in a DOS
subdirectory, your CONFIG.SYS entry might become:

```
DEVICE=C:\DOS\ANSI.SYS
```

Remember: After you change the CONFIG.SYS file, you
must restart your computer for the change to take effect.

To use the ANSI.SYS-enhanced capabilities of your screen
and keyboard from your batch files, you must use either
the DOS command ECHO or the DOS command PROMPT
to send escape sequences to the device driver.

An *escape sequence* is a unique character combination that
begins with the ASCII escape character (ASCII 27). The
ANSI.SYS device driver supports several escape sequences to set your screen color, set the cursor position, or
redefine keys on your keyboard.

To begin, let's use ANSI.SYS to set screen colors. The
ANSI.SYS escape sequence to set your screen's color is:

Escape[colorm

where *Escape* is the ASCII escape character and *color* is
one of the color values defined in the following table.

COLOR VALUES SUPPORTED BY ANSI.SYS

Color Value	Color
0	Default color (black and white)
1	Bold text attribute
2*	Low-intensity text attribute
3*	Italic text attribute
4	Underscore on for IBM monochrome; un-derscore color (blue) for VGA
5	Blinking text attribute
6*	Rapid-blinking text attribute
7	Reverse-video text attribute

(continued)

continued

Color Value	Color
8	Concealed text attribute
30	Black foreground
31	Red foreground
32	Green foreground
33	Yellow foreground
34	Blue foreground
35	Magenta foreground
36	Cyan foreground
37	White foreground
40	Black background
41	Red background
42	Green background
43	Yellow background
44	Blue background
45	Magenta background
46	Cyan background
47	White background
48*	Subscript
49*	Superscript

* Not operative on VGA.

Note: Not all values are supported in all versions of ANSI.SYS.

For example, the ANSI.SYS escape sequence:

```
Escape[31m
```

sets the screen foreground color to red. Likewise, the sequence:

```
Escape[42m
```

selects a green background. Using the PROMPT $e metacharacter, a batch file, named CYANBG.BAT, sets the screen background color to cyan:

```
PROMPT $e[46m
PROMPT [$p]
CLS
```

The PROMPT $e metacharacter directs PROMPT to write the ASCII escape character. The first command sets the screen color to cyan, while the second PROMPT command resets the system prompt to the current drive and directory, both displayed within square brackets. The CLS command simply clears the screen display, setting the screen's background color to cyan.

In a similar manner, the batch file BLUEFG.BAT uses the PROMPT command to set the screen's foreground color to blue:

```
PROMPT $e[34m
PROMPT [$p]
CLS
```

If you run this batch file, the ANSI.SYS device driver changes your screen's foreground to blue, leaving the screen background color unchanged.

As you can see, the batch files CYANBG.BAT and BLUEFG.BAT are almost identical—the only difference is the color value. Therefore, we can create a single batch file, named SCRCOLOR.BAT, that sets the screen-color attributes based on the batch parameter %1. In this case, the batch file becomes:

```
IF "%1"=="" GOTO DONE
PROMPT $e[%1m
PROMPT [$p]
CLS
:DONE
```

To set your screen color, simply specify the color value as a batch-file parameter. For example, the command line:

```
C> SCRCOLOR 42
```

sets the screen's background color to green. DOS simply places the value 42 into the batch file (replacing %1), yielding the escape sequence:

```
Escape[42m
```

You might be wondering when your batch files would use the bold, blinking, or reverse-video attributes.

Consider an application that displays the message:

```
About to delete FILENAME.EXT
Press any key to continue . . .
```

Earlier in this reference you learned how to use the computer's built-in "bell" to get the user's attention before displaying a message with PAUSE. The following batch file, named DELETE.BAT, uses the blinking text attribute to get the user's attention:

```
ECHO OFF
IF "%1"=="" GOTO DONE
REM Set text attribute to blinking.
REM Must turn ECHO ON for prompt command to
REM change the text attribute.
PROMPT $e[5m
ECHO ON
ECHO OFF
CLS
PROMPT [$p]
REM Displaying warning message
ECHO About to delete %1
PAUSE
DEL %1
PROMPT $e[0m
REM Restore default color. Again, turn ECHO ON.
ECHO ON
ECHO OFF
PROMPT [$p]
:DONE
```

Although this batch file displays a blinking message as specified, when it completes execution, it sets the screen color back to its default setting. If you have used the ANSI.SYS device driver to set your screen's color, the color is lost.

As a solution, a batch file, named SCRCOLOR.BAT, can define the three named parameters—TEXTATTR, FOREGROUND, and BACKGROUND—as follows:

```
IF "%1"=="" GOTO DONE
PROMPT $e[%1m
```

```
PROMPT [$p]
CLS
ECHO OFF
REM Set the named parameters TextAttr, ForeGround,
REM and BackGround
IF "%1"=="0" SET TEXTATTR=0
IF "%1"=="1" SET TEXTATTR=1
IF "%1"=="2" SET TEXTATTR=2
IF "%1"=="3" SET TEXTATTR=3
IF "%1"=="4" SET TEXTATTR=4
IF "%1"=="5" SET TEXTATTR=5
IF "%1"=="6" SET TEXTATTR=6
IF "%1"=="7" SET TEXTATTR=7
IF "%1"=="8" SET TEXTATTR=8
IF "%1"=="30" SET FOREGROUND=30
IF "%1"=="31" SET FOREGROUND=31
IF "%1"=="32" SET FOREGROUND=32
IF "%1"=="33" SET FOREGROUND=33
IF "%1"=="34" SET FOREGROUND=34
IF "%1"=="35" SET FOREGROUND=35
IF "%1"=="36" SET FOREGROUND=36
IF "%1"=="37" SET FOREGROUND=37
IF "%1"=="40" SET BACKGROUND=40
IF "%1"=="41" SET BACKGROUND=41
IF "%1"=="42" SET BACKGROUND=42
IF "%1"=="43" SET BACKGROUND=43
IF "%1"=="44" SET BACKGROUND=44
IF "%1"=="45" SET BACKGROUND=45
IF "%1"=="46" SET BACKGROUND=46
IF "%1"=="47" SET BACKGROUND=47
IF "%1"=="48" SET BACKGROUND=48
IF "%1"=="49" SET BACKGROUND=49
:DONE
```

As you can see, depending on the color value that you specify as the first parameter of SCRCOLOR.BAT, the batch
file defines one of the three named parameters accordingly.

When you create another batch file, such as
DELETE.BAT, which changes screen attributes, the
batch file can test to see if these named parameters exist,
and if they do, it can restore the previous screen colors.

```
ECHO OFF
IF "%1"=="" GOTO DONE
REM Set text attribute to blinking.
REM Must turn ECHO ON for prompt command to
REM change the text attribute.
PROMPT $e[5m
ECHO ON
ECHO OFF
CLS
PROMPT [$p]
REM Displaying warning message
ECHO About to delete %1
PAUSE
DEL %1
REM Restore default color. Again, turn ECHO ON.
ECHO ON
IF NOT "%TEXTATTR%"=="" PROMPT $e[%TEXTATTR%m
IF NOT "%FOREGROUND%"=="" PROMPT $e[%FOREGROUND%m
IF NOT "%BACKGROUND%"=="" PROMPT $e[%BACKGROUND%m
ECHO OFF
CLS
PROMPT [$p]
:DONE
```

As briefly discussed, the DOS command ECHO also lets
your batch files send escape sequences to the ANSI.SYS
device driver. The easiest way to create a batch file that
uses ECHO to write escape sequences is with Edlin. In this
manner, you can create the batch file SCRERASE.BAT,
which uses the ANSI.SYS escape sequence:

Escape[2J

to erase the screen display, placing the cursor at the
screen's upper left (home) position. As discussed before,
run Edlin with the filename, as follows:

```
C> EDLIN SCRERASE.BAT
```

Edlin displays:

```
C> EDLIN SCRERASE.BAT
New file
*
```

Next, using I, the Edlin insert command, type the word
ECHO and press the Spacebar once:

```
C> EDLIN SCRERASE.BAT
New file
*I
        1:* ECHO
```

Next, you must enter the ANSI.SYS escape sequence to
clear the screen. To enter the ASCII escape character, hold
down the Ctrl key and press V, and then release the Ctrl
key and type a left bracket:

```
C> EDLIN SCRERASE.BAT
New file
*I
        1:* ECHO ^V[
```

Next, type another left bracket, and then type *2J*:

```
C> EDLIN SCRERASE.BAT
New file
*I
        1:* ECHO ^V[[2J
```

Edlin uses the characters ^V[as the ASCII escape character. Press Enter and then Ctrl-C to exit Edlin's insert mode.
Save the batch file using E, the Edlin exit command. When
you run SCRERASE, the ECHO command writes the
ANSI.SYS escape sequence that clears your screen. (Admittedly, you can easily use the DOS command CLS. The
purpose of the batch file SCRERASE.BAT was to teach
you how to use ECHO to echo an escape sequence.)

DOS 5 provides EDIT, a full-screen text (ASCII) editor
that is much easier to use than Edlin. However, EDIT uses
a unique key combination to generate the ASCII escape
character: Hold down the Ctrl key and type *P* (nothing displays on the screen, and the cursor does not move), and
then release the Ctrl key and press the Esc key (a left-point-
ing arrow displays and the cursor moves one position to
the right). Refer to the MS-DOS 5 User's Guide and Reference for full details on the use of EDIT.

In addition to setting the foreground and background colors of your screen and erasing your screen display, the

ANSI.SYS device driver allows your batch files to control the cursor's position on your screen. After you use the ANSI.SYS device driver to position the cursor, the next output occurs at that position.

The following table defines the five ANSI.SYS cursor-positioning routines:

Escape Sequence	Result
Escape[NumRowsA	Move cursor up
Escape[NumRowsB	Move cursor down
Escape[NumRowsC	Move cursor right
Escape[NumRowsD	Move cursor left
Escape[Row;ColH	Set cursor at the Row, Col position

Most screens use 25 rows and 80 columns. The extreme upper left screen position is 1, 1—that is, row 1, column 1. The extreme lower right screen position is 25, 80. A batch file, named CURPOS.BAT, uses the ANSI escape sequences:

```
Escape[1;1H
Escape[5;5H
Escape[10;10H
Escape[20;20H
```

to display messages at the row and column positions (1, 1), (5, 5), (10, 10), and (20, 20). The batch file uses the ECHO batch-file command to set the cursor position:

```
ECHO OFF
CLS
ECHO Escape[1;1HRow 1, Column 1
ECHO Escape[5;5HRow 5, Column 5
ECHO Escape[10;10HRow 10, Column 10
ECHO Escape[20;20HRow 20, Column 20
```

Because it is difficult to display the ASCII escape character within a text, this batch file uses the word *Escape* each time you need to include the ASCII escape character. If you are using Edlin to create your batch files, use the ^V[character combination in place of each *Escape*.

Earlier in this reference, we created the batch file
HELPDOS.BAT, which displayed on-line help for each
DOS command. Using the ANSI.SYS device driver, you
can change the batch file to display command names centered on the screen in bold text and to display the actual
help text in a distinct foreground color.

This batch-file fragment illustrates the use of the
ANSI.SYS device driver for help on the DOS command
CLS:

```
ECHO OFF
CLS
REM Set all attributes off.
ECHO Escape[0m
REM Select bold text.
ECHO Escape[1m
REM Center the word CLS.
ECHO Escape[1;35HCLS
REM Select blue color for text.
ECHO Escape[34m
ECHO Escape[3;10HCommand Type: Internal
ECHO Escape[5;10HFunction: Erases the screen
ECHO Escape[5;37H display, placing the
ECHO Escape[6;20Hcursor at the upper left, or
ECHO Escape[6;48H home, position.
ECHO Escape[8;10HExample: CLS
```

In this case, the fragment first disables any currently set attributes to avoid potential color conflicts. Then, the batch
file uses the ANSI.SYS device driver to set the text attribute to bold and then to center the CLS command name.
Next, the batch file selects the foreground color and displays the help text. As you can see, the batch file uses the
escape sequence:

Escape[Row;ColH

to display each line of help information starting at column
10 (continued lines begin in column 20). After the batch
file displays the help text, the batch file could use the
ANSI.SYS driver to reset the video attributes to their normal state. (Later in this reference, you will learn how to
create and use menus from within your batch files. At that

time, you will use the ANSI.SYS cursor-positioning escape
sequences extensively.)

The ANSI.SYS device driver enhances both screen and
keyboard capabilities. You have just used the ANSI.SYS
driver to clear the screen, set foreground and background
colors, and position the cursor. To enhance your
keyboard's capabilities, ANSI.SYS lets you redefine keys.
Most users use ANSI.SYS to assign character strings to the
function keys. Remember, in DOS 5, function keys F1
through F10 are used by DOSKEY; earlier versions of
DOS use function keys F1 through F6 for command-line
editing.

Each key on your keyboard has a unique value associated
with it; this value is called a *scan code*. The keys F7
through F10 use the scan-code values 65, 66, 67, and 68,
respectively. To assign a character string to one of these
function keys, your ANSI.SYS escape sequence becomes:

Escape[0;Scancode;"string"p

For example, to assign the DOS command VER to the function key F7, your command line becomes:

```
Escape[0;65;"VER"p
```

Likewise, to assign the CLS command to the F10 function
key, the ANSI escape sequence becomes:

```
Escape[0;68;"CLS"p
```

A batch file, named DEFKEY.BAT, uses the ANSI.SYS
keyboard-reassignment escape sequence to define a function key on the keyboard:

```
IF "%1"=="" GOTO DONE
IF "%2"=="" GOTO DONE
ECHO Escape[0;%1;"%2"p
:DONE
```

This batch file uses the *%1* batch parameter to determine
the key to define, and it uses the *%2* batch parameter to determine the value to assign to the key. For example, to

assign the CLS command to the F10 function key, your command line becomes:

```
C> DEFKEY 68 CLS
```

As you can see, the batch file substitutes the values *68* and *CLS* into the escape sequence:

```
ECHO Escape[0;68;"CLS"p
```

In many cases, you will want to assign several words to a key. For example:

```
C> DEFKEY 68 DIR *.* /P
```

To do so, simply change the batch file DEFKEY.BAT to use the batch parameters %1 through %9, as follows:

```
IF "%1"=="" GOTO DONE
IF "%2"=="" GOTO DONE
ECHO Escape[0;%1;"%2 %3 %4 %5 %6 %7 %8 %9"p
:DONE
```

By assigning commonly used commands to the function keys, you can save time and keystrokes. Note, though, that if you use DOSKEY, it has predefined actions already assigned to each of the first 10 function keys.

Remember: After you create the batch file DEFKEY.BAT, you can run it from AUTOEXEC.BAT by using either COMMAND /C or the CALL batch-file command. In so doing, your keyboard definitions are active each time your system starts.

Now you've had a glimpse of what can be done with keyboard reassignment and how it can be accomplished. Be aware that the first parameter in these examples consists of a 0 followed by a semicolon and the scan-code value when the scan code consists of an ASCII extended value. For scan codes that do *not* use ASCII extended values, the zero and its semicolon must not be used.

The ASCII extended scan codes and their definitions are:

Scan Codes	Definitions
15	Shift-Tab
16–25	Alt- q, w, e, r, t, y, u, i, o, p

(continued)

continued

Scan Codes	Definitions
30–38	Alt- a, s, d, f, g, h, j, k, l
44–50	Alt- z, x, c, v, b, n, m
59–68	F1–F10
71	Home
72	Cursor Up
73	Page Up
75	Cursor Left
77	Cursor Right
79	End
80	Cursor Down
81	Page Down
82	Insert
83	Delete
84–93	Shift-F1 through Shift-F10
94–103	Ctrl-F1 through Ctrl-F10
104–113	Alt-F1 through Alt-F10

USING *DEBUG* TO UNLEASH YOUR BATCH-PROCESSING POTENTIAL

All the DOS commands were written by computer programmers using a programming language such as C or Pascal. Only a small portion of the 60 million DOS users are programmers. To achieve total control of your batch files, you need to develop a few simple programs—even if you're not a programmer. For DOS users, the DEBUG command provides all the capabilities needed to write simple programs that enhance batch-file capabilities. DEBUG is a programmer's utility that helps programmers find errors, or "bugs," in their programs. Although most of us won't use DEBUG to find program errors, we can use it to create simple programs. DEBUG intimidates many users because they view DEBUG as a utility designed exclusively for programmers, and because DEBUG requires the entry of program instructions in assembly language.

However, if you follow the examples as they appear in this reference, you will find DEBUG very easy to use. You will create several programs using DEBUG. The examples explain each step you must type. If you take a few minutes to type these programs, you will greatly enhance your batch-file capabilities.

DEBUG* is an external DOS command that resides on disk:

C> `DIR DEBUG.EXE`

```
 Volume in drive C is DOS 5
 Volume Serial Number is 3A2F-18E9
 Directory of  C:\DOS

DEBUG     EXE      20506 12-13-90   4:09a
       1 File(s)         20506 bytes
                      21166080 bytes free

-
```

When you execute DEBUG, you will specify, on the command line, the name of the file that DEBUG is to create:

C> `DEBUG FILENAME.EXT`

To begin, let's create a program, named SCRPRINT.COM, that prints the current contents of your screen display. Assume, for example, that a program in your batch file displays important data on the screen. To ensure that the user sees this information, your batch file can run SCRPRINT (when the program completes execution) to print the screen's contents.

To begin, execute DEBUG with the SCRPRINT.COM filename:

C> `DEBUG SCRPRINT.COM`

DEBUG will respond with:

```
C> DEBUG SCRPRINT.COM
File not found

-
```

*Note that in releases prior to DOS 5, the full name of DEBUG is DEBUG.COM.

The message *File not found* tells you that SCRPRINT.COM did not previously exist on disk. The dash (-) is DEBUG's prompt.

Type the command *A 100* and press the Enter key:

```
C> DEBUG SCRPRINT.COM
File not found

-A 100
5AFF:0100
```

The A 100 command tells DEBUG that you want to enter program commands at the hexadecimal offset 100. Each time DOS runs a program, DOS begins execution at this offset—so that's where we will place our instructions. All the programs you will create using DEBUG will begin using the A 100 command.

Consider the manner in which DEBUG displays your program's line numbers. In this case, the rightmost number is 0100—because we told DEBUG to begin at offset 100. The number your computer displays to the left of 0100 might differ from the number shown here. The leftmost number depends on where DOS starts DEBUG in memory. Depending on your version of DOS as well as on the programs you have installed, this value can vary. Type the command *INT 5* and press Enter:

```
C> DEBUG SCRPRINT.COM
File not found

-A 100
5AFF:0100 INT 5
5AFF:0102
```

The INT 5 command directs your computer to print its screen contents.

It's as easy as that! Next, you must include two more instructions that tell DOS to end the program. First, type *MOV AH, 4C* and press Enter. Second, type *INT 21* and press Enter. Your program is complete.

You must now tell DEBUG to save the program's contents on disk. To start the save process for the program, press Enter. DEBUG displays its prompt, as follows:

```
C> DEBUG SCRPRINT.COM
File not found

-A 100
5AFF:0100 INT 5
5AFF:0102 MOV AH, 4C
5AFF:0104 INT 21
5AFF:0106
-
```

Next, issue the DEBUG command *R CX*, and DEBUG responds:

```
-R CX
CX 0000
:
```

CX is a register or storage location built into your computer. Before DEBUG can write the program on disk, DEBUG must know how large the program is. Therefore, you must place the program size in the CX register. Find the value that corresponds to the last line number in the program:

```
C> DEBUG SCRPRINT.COM
File not found

-A 100
5AFF:0100 INT 5
5AFF:0102 MOV AH, 4C
5AFF:0104 INT 21
5AFF:0106  ———— Last program line
-R CX
CX 0000
:
```

and subtract the beginning offset from that value (for example, "0106 minus 0100 equals 6"). In this case, your program is 6 bytes long. Type the value *6* at DEBUG's colon prompt for the CX value. When you press Enter, DEBUG displays its command prompt:

```
C> DEBUG SCRPRINT.COM
File not found
```

```
-A 100
5AFF:0100 INT 5
5AFF:0102 MOV AH, 4C
5AFF:0104 INT 21
5AFF:0106
-R CX
CX 0000
:6
-
```

To save the file on disk, you issue the DEBUG write command, W.

```
C> DEBUG SCRPRINT.COM
File not found

-A 100
5AFF:0100 INT 5
5AFF:0102 MOV AH, 4C
5AFF:0104 INT 21
5AFF:0106
-R CX
CX 0000
:6
-W
Writing 0006 bytes
```

After DEBUG saves the file on disk, use the DEBUG quit command, Q, to return to the DOS prompt:

```
C> DEBUG SCRPRINT.COM
File not found

-A 100
5AFF:0100 INT 5
5AFF:0102 MOV AH, 4C
5AFF:0104 INT 21
5AFF:0106
-R CX
CX 0000
:6
-W
Writing 0006 bytes
-Q

C>
```

If you run the program SCRPRINT from the DOS prompt, DOS prints the current screen contents. A directory listing of the file reveals:

```
C> DIR SCRPRINT.COM
 Volume in drive C is DOS 5
 Volume Serial Number is 3A2F-18E9
 Directory of  C:\BATCH

SCRPRINT COM          6 05-11-91  12:11p
        1 File(s)             6 bytes
                    21155840 bytes free
```

As you can see, the size of the file is 6 bytes.

In a similar manner, the program REBOOT.COM reboots DOS:

```
C> DEBUG REBOOT.COM
File not found

-A 100
584B:0100 MOV AX, 40
584B:0103 MOV DS, AX
584B:0105 MOV AX, 1234
584B:0108 MOV [72], AX
584B:010B JMP FFFF:0
584B:0110
-R CX
CX 0000
:10
-W
Writing 0010 bytes
-Q

C>
```

REBOOT.COM uses the bootstrap program that starts your computer when you turn its power on. The PC bootstrap program examines the memory location 0472H to see if it contains the value 1234. If it does contain the value, the PC performs a Ctrl-Alt-Del system restart. REBOOT.COM places the value 1234 into the correct memory location and then issues the command JMP to branch to the bootstrap program. The following program includes comments that explain REBOOT.COM's processing:

```
C> DEBUG REBOOT.COM
File not found
```

```
-A 100
584B:0100 MOV AX, 40     ; Segment address of 0472H
584B:0103 MOV DS, AX      ; Assign address to data segment
584B:0105 MOV AX, 1234    ; 1234 tells bootstrap to "reboot"
584B:0108 MOV [72], AX    ; Move value into memory
584B:010B JMP FFFF:0      ; Jump to bootstrap program
584B:0110
-R CX
CX 0000
:10
-W
Writing 0010 bytes
-Q

C>
```

In this case, if you run REBOOT from the DOS prompt,
your system restarts. Let's consider an application where
you might need a batch file to reboot DOS. Many users use
RAM disks in memory to provide a fast disk drive. Depending on your version of DOS, you will use either the file
RAMDRIVE.SYS or the file VDISK.SYS to create a RAM
drive. A RAM drive is a disk drive that you instruct DOS
to create in your computer's RAM (random-access memory). After you create a RAM drive, the DOS commands
can reference the drive using a single drive letter and
colon—exactly as they would to access a floppy disk or a
hard disk.

Because a RAM drive resides in your computer's memory,
it does not have the mechanical constraints of a floppy disk
or a hard disk. As a result, the RAM drive is much faster.
A RAM disk gives you a fast temporary storage location
for your files. However, when you turn off your computer,
the contents of your RAM drive are lost.

Assuming your version of DOS uses the file RAMDRIVE.SYS,
you create a RAM drive by installing the RAMDRIVE.SYS device driver in memory using the CONFIG.SYS DEVICE=
entry. For example, the entry:

```
DEVICE=RAMDRIVE.SYS
```

creates a RAM drive using the 64 KB default size. To create a RAM drive of 256 KB, use the entry:

```
DEVICE=RAMDRIVE.SYS 256
```

Note: You must reboot your system for CONFIG.SYS changes to take effect.

Many users install a RAM disk for their daily computer operations, only to have to remove the RAM disk later when they run a large application program that consumes a large amount of memory. Remember: A 256 KB RAM disk consumes 256 KB of memory.

Each time the user needs to remove the RAM disk from memory, the user must edit the file CONFIG.SYS by removing the DEVICE=RAMDRIVE entry. Next, the user must reboot. If the user again wants to install the RAM disk, the user must again edit CONFIG.SYS and again reboot DOS.

Rather than continually performing this edit–reboot cycle, you can create a batch file, named RAMDRIVE.BAT, that performs this task for you. For example, to install the RAM disk, you run the batch file as:

```
C> RAMDRIVE INSTALL 128
```

In this case, the batch file installs a RAM drive capable of storing 128 KB. To later unload the RAM, run the batch file as:

```
C> RAMDRIVE UNLOAD
```

In either case, the batch file edits CONFIG.SYS for you, rebooting DOS for your changes to take effect, as follows:

```
ECHO OFF
IF "%1"=="INSTALL" GOTO INSTALL_DISK
IF "%1"=="UNLOAD" GOTO UNLOAD_DISK
GOTO DONE
:INSTALL_DISK
REM Install the RAM disk by adding the DEVICE=RAMDRIVE
REM entry in CONFIG.SYS. Use %2 to determine the
REM size of the RAM disk. After CONFIG.SYS is
REM updated, reboot.
```

```
IF NOT EXIST \CONFIG.SYS GOTO ADD_ENTRY
REM
REM Remove all lines in CONFIG.SYS containing RAMDRIVE.
REM
TYPE \CONFIG.SYS | FIND /V "RAMDRIVE"> \CONFIG.NEW
DEL \CONFIG.SYS
REM
REM Append the RAMDRIVE entry to CONFIG.SYS.
REM
:ADD_ENTRY
ECHO DEVICE=RAMDRIVE.SYS %2 >> \CONFIG.NEW
REN \CONFIG.NEW CONFIG.SYS
REBOOT
GOTO DONE
:UNLOAD_DISK
REM Remove the RAM disk by removing the RAMDRIVE entry
REM from CONFIG.SYS and rebooting.
IF NOT EXIST \CONFIG.SYS GOTO DONE
REM
REM Remove all lines in CONFIG.SYS containing RAMDRIVE.
REM
TYPE \CONFIG.SYS | FIND /V "RAMDRIVE" > \CONFIG.NEW
DEL \CONFIG.SYS
REN \CONFIG.NEW CONFIG.SYS
REBOOT
:DONE
```

The ECHO batch-file command following the label
:ADD_ENTRY assumes that the file RAMDRIVE.SYS
can be found in the root directory. If that is not the case,
you must provide the appropriate drive and/or subdirectory name as a part of the filename—for example,
c:\dos\ramdrive.sys.

In the routine starting with the label :ADD_ENTRY, the
GOTO DONE statement following the REBOOT statement
is intended never to be executed, because the system
should reboot. However, if the REBOOT program does not
exist or cannot be found, the GOTO DONE statement will
ensure that the remainder of the batch file is not acciden-
tally run.

Next, a program, named GETYORN.COM, gets keystrokes from the user until the user presses either the Y key
or the N key. After GETYORN.COM gets a valid key, it returns the key as an EXIT status value. Therefore, your program can use the conditions:

```
GETYORN
IF ERRORLEVEL 89 GOTO YES
IF ERRORLEVEL 78 GOTO NO
```

to process the yes or no response. Notice that the batch file
first tests for the higher exit status (89).

Remember: The IF ERRORLEVEL condition returns a
value of true when the specified value is greater than or
equal to the exit status. If you place the test for an exit status of 78 first, DOS always executes the corresponding
commands because both keys return values greater than or
equal to 78.

The following program implements GETYORN.COM:

```
C> DEBUG GETYORN.COM
File not found

-A 100
5B10:0100 MOV AH, 08
5B10:0102 INT 21
5B10:0104 CMP AL, 59     ; Did user press Y?
5B10:0106 JZ  010E
5B10:0108 CMP AL, 4E     ; Did user press N?
5B10:010A JZ  010E
5B10:010C JMP 0100       ; Loop to get valid character
5B10:010E MOV AH, 4C
5B10:0110 INT 21         ; End program
5B10:0112
-R CX
CX 0000
:12
-W
Writing 0012 bytes
-Q

C>
```

As you can see, the program is slightly more complex than those in the previous two examples. However, if you type it exactly as it appears, you will have no problems.

For programmers wanting to understand the assembly-language code that GETYORN.COM uses, the following listing includes a short explanation:

```
C> DEBUG GETYORN.COM
File not found

-A 100
5B10:0100 MOV AH, 08  ; DOS Get character service
5B10:0102 INT 21      ; Call the service
5B10:0104 CMP AL, 59  ; Did user press Y?
5B10:0106 JZ  010E    ; Valid letter, jump to end program
5B10:0108 CMP AL, 4E  ; Did user press N?
5B10:010A JZ  010E    ; Valid letter, jump to end program
5B10:010C JMP 0100    ; Loop to get valid character
5B10:010E MOV AH, 4C  ; DOS End Program service
5B10:0110 INT 21      ; Call service, ending program
5B10:0112
-R CX
CX 0000
:12
-W
Writing 0012 bytes
-Q

C>
```

After you create GETYORN.COM, you can put it to use immediately in a batch file, named DELETEYN.BAT. This batch file uses the DOS commands FOR and DEL, allowing you to selectively delete files. Actually, DELETEYN.BAT creates a temporary batch file that it uses to delete files. When the temporary batch file named ERASEIT.BAT is no longer needed, DELETEYN.BAT deletes it:

```
ECHO OFF
REM Create the temporary batch file ERASEIT.BAT that
REM prompts the user to keep or delete a file.
REM If the user presses Y, the batch file deletes
REM the file. If the user presses N, the batch file
REM leaves the file on disk.
```

```
REM Use ECHO and DOS redirection to create the
REM batch file.
ECHO ECHO Do you want to delete %%1? > ERASEIT.BAT
ECHO GETYORN >> ERASEIT.BAT
ECHO IF ERRORLEVEL 89 DEL %%1 >> ERASEIT.BAT

REM Now that the file ERASEIT.BAT exists on disk,
REM use it within the FOR loop.

FOR %%I IN (%1) DO CALL ERASEIT %%I

REM The batch file ERASEIT.BAT is no longer needed.
DEL ERASEIT.BAT
```

This batch file provides much information. It shows you that you can create a batch file from within a batch file and that your batch file can then run it. Next, examine the three lines that actually create the batch file:

```
ECHO ECHO Do you want to delete %%1? > ERASEIT.BAT
ECHO GETYORN >> ERASEIT.BAT
ECHO IF ERRORLEVEL 89 DEL %%1 >> ERASEIT.BAT
```

The batch file uses the DOS output redirection operator (>) to create a batch file, named ERASEIT.BAT. The next two commands use the DOS append redirection operator (>>) to add commands to the batch file. Notice the use of the double percent signs in *%%1*. As you will recall, each time DOS detects the *%1* in a batch file, DOS substitutes the value of the first batch parameter.

In this case, however, we don't want DOS to substitute a parameter; instead, we want DOS to write the characters *%1* to the batch file ERASEIT.BAT. If you use the double percent signs, DOS does not perform the substitution, but DOS does write the characters *%1* to the batch file ERASEIT.BAT, as intended. This lets ERASEIT.BAT support batch parameters.

The primary processing in a batch file, named DELETEYN.BAT, is the FOR loop, which passes each filename to the batch file ERASEIT.BAT. Each time the

FOR loop calls the batch file, ERASEIT.BAT asks the user if the specified filename should be deleted. The batch file then uses the program GETYORN.COM, which we just created, to determine the user's response. If the user presses Y (for yes), the batch file deletes the file. If the user presses N (for no), ERASEIT.BAT completes execution and the FOR loop repeats.

If you run the batch file DELETEYN.BAT as:

```
C> DELETEYN *.*
```

the batch file allows you to selectively delete any file in the current directory on your default disk drive.

In a manner similar to the program GETYORN.COM, a program, named F1TOF10.COM, returns the keyboard scan-code values 59 through 68. These scan-code values correspond to the function keys F1 through F10. The following program implements F1TOF10.COM:

```
C> DEBUG F1TOF10.COM
File not found

-A 100
5B10:0100 MOV AH, 08
5B10:0102 INT 21
5B10:0104 CMP AL, 0
5B10:0106 JNZ 0100
5B10:0108 MOV AH, 08
5B10:010A INT 21
5B10:010C CMP AL, 3B
5B10:010E JL  0100
5B10:0110 CMP AL, 44
5B10:0112 JG 0100
5B10:0114 MOV AH, 4C
5B10:0116 INT 21
5B10:0118
-R CX
CX 0000
:18
-W
Writing 0018 bytes
-Q

C>
```

The following listing explains the program's processing:

```
C> DEBUG F1TOF10.COM
File not found

-A 100
5B10:0100 MOV AH, 08    ; Get key service
5B10:0102 INT 21        ; Call the service
5B10:0104 CMP AL, 0     ; AL=0 if function key
5B10:0106 JNZ 0100      ; Wasn't 0, try again
5B10:0108 MOV AH, 08    ; Next, get the scan code
5B10:010A INT 21        ; Call the service
5B10:010C CMP AL, 3B    ; Compare scan code to 3B (F1)
5B10:010E JL  0100      ; Too low, try again
5B10:0110 CMP AL, 44    ; Compare scan code to 44 (F10)
5B10:0112 JG 0100       ; Too high, try again
5B10:0114 MOV AH, 4C    ; End the program service
5B10:0116 INT 21        ; Call service, ending program
5B10:0118
-R CX
CX 0000
:18
-W
Writing 0018 bytes
-Q

C>
```

The batch file DOSMENU.BAT displays the menu:

F1 - Display DIRectory listing
F2 - Display DOS version number
F3 - Display Disk volume label
F4 - Quit

If the user presses F1, the batch file displays a directory listing. If the user presses F2, the program displays the current version number. If the user presses F3, the batch file displays the current volume label. The batch file continues this processing until the user presses F4 to quit. The listing for DOSMENU.BAT is:

```
ECHO OFF
CLS
:LOOP
ECHO F1 - Display DIRectory listing
ECHO F2 - Display DOS version number
```

```
ECHO F3 - Display Disk volume label
ECHO F4 - Quit
REM Get user response
:GET_KEY
F1TOF10
IF ERRORLEVEL 63 GOTO GET_KEY
IF ERRORLEVEL 62 GOTO DONE
IF ERRORLEVEL 61 IF NOT ERRORLEVEL 62 VOL
IF ERRORLEVEL 60 IF NOT ERRORLEVEL 61 VER
IF ERRORLEVEL 59 IF NOT ERRORLEVEL 60 DIR
GOTO LOOP
:DONE
```

The batch file first displays the menu and then runs the program F1TOF10 to get a function-key response. If the user
presses a function key from F5 through F10, the batch file
loops back to get a valid key. If the user presses the F4 key
(scan code 62), the batch file ends. Notice the use of the two
IF commands to test if an exit status is a specific value. By
using two IF commands in this manner, the batch file can test
whether the exit-status value is 61, 60, or 59, as opposed to a
value that is greater than or equal to one of these values.

Finally, a program, named GETARROW.COM, waits for
the user to press the Up arrow key, the Down arrow key, or
the Enter key. The program returns an exit status of 72 for
an Up arrow and a value of 80 for a Down arrow. If the
user presses Enter, the batch file returns 13. Here is the
GETARROW.COM program:

```
C> DEBUG GETARROW.COM
File not found

-A 100
5B10:0100 MOV AH, 8
5B10:0102 INT 21
5B10:0104 CMP AL, D
5B10:0106 JZ   11A
5B10:0108 CMP AL, 0
5B10:010A JNZ  100
5B10:010C MOV AH, 8
5B10:010E INT 21
5B10:0110 CMP AL, 48
5B10:0112 JZ   11A
```

```
5B10:0114 CMP AL, 50
5B10:0116 JZ  11A
5B10:0118 JMP 100
5B10:011A MOV AH, 4C
5B10:011C INT 21
5B10:011E
-R CX
CX 0000
:1E
-W
Writing 001E bytes
-Q

C>
```

A batch file, named ARROW.BAT, displays a menu similar to that of the previous program:

Display DIRectory
Display DOS version
Display volume label
Quit

In this case, the batch file uses the ANSI.SYS device driver to highlight the current menu choice. As the user presses the Up or the Down direction (arrow) key, the current choice changes. When the user presses Enter, the batch file executes the current choice:

```
ECHO OFF
SET CURRENT=DIR
:LOOP
CLS
IF %CURRENT%==DIR ECHO Escape[1mDisplay DIRectory
IF NOT %CURRENT%==DIR ECHO Escape[0mDisplay DIRectory
IF %CURRENT%==VER ECHO Escape[1mDisplay DOS version
IF NOT %CURRENT%==VER ECHO Escape[0mDisplay DOS version
IF %CURRENT%==VOL ECHO Escape[1mDisplay volume label
IF NOT %CURRENT%==VOL ECHO Escape[0mDisplay volume label
IF %CURRENT%==QUIT ECHO Escape[1mQuit
IF NOT %CURRENT%==QUIT ECHO Escape[0mQuit
GETARROW
IF ERRORLEVEL 80 GOTO DOWN_ARROW
IF ERRORLEVEL 72 GOTO UP_ARROW
IF %CURRENT%==DIR DIR
IF %CURRENT%==VER VER
```

```
IF %CURRENT%==VOL VOL
IF %CURRENT%==QUIT GOTO DONE
PAUSE
GOTO LOOP

:UP_ARROW
IF NOT %CURRENT%==DIR GOTO UP_ _VER
SET CURRENT=QUIT
GOTO LOOP
:UP_ _VER
IF NOT %CURRENT%==VER GOTO UP_ _VOL
SET CURRENT=DIR
GOTO LOOP
:UP_ _VOL
IF NOT %CURRENT%==VOL GOTO UP_ _QUIT
SET CURRENT=VER
GOTO LOOP
:UP_ _QUIT
SET CURRENT=VOL
GOTO LOOP

:DOWN_ARROW
IF NOT %CURRENT%==DIR GOTO DOWN_ _VER
SET CURRENT=VER
GOTO LOOP
:DOWN_ _VER
IF NOT %CURRENT%==VER GOTO DOWN_ _VOL
SET CURRENT=VOL
GOTO LOOP
:DOWN_ _VOL
IF NOT %CURRENT%==VOL GOTO DOWN_ _QUIT
SET CURRENT=QUIT
GOTO LOOP
:DOWN_ _QUIT
SET CURRENT=DIR
GOTO LOOP

:DONE
ECHO Escape[0m
SET CURRENT=
```

The batch file's menu-manipulation capabilities are normally restricted to programs written in languages such as Pascal or C. This batch file keeps track of the current option, using the named parameter CURRENT. When the batch file begins execution, it uses the DOS command SET to assign to the named parameter the value DIR. If you look at the menu that ARROW.BAT displays, DIR is the first choice. Next, the batch file uses the IF batch-file command to determine the current option. The batch file uses the ANSI.SYS escape sequence *Escape[1m* to display the current option with a bold attribute. The batch file uses the escape sequence *Escape[0m* to display all the other options with a normal attribute.

Next, the batch file uses the program GETARROW.COM, which we just created, to get either an Up or a Down direction key or the Enter key. If the user presses Enter, the batch file uses the named parameter CURRENT to determine the command to execute. If the user instead presses either the Up or the Down direction key, the batch file determines the new current option and redisplays the menu.

When the user finally selects the Quit option, the batch file resets the video attribute to normal and removes the named parameter CURRENT from the DOS environment.

Admittedly, our batch-file menu options are quite basic; however, ARROW.BAT illustrates the amount of programming you can actually perform using DOS batch files.

USING THE ASCII EXTENDED CHARACTER SET

The computer represents all the characters, numbers, and symbols that DOS displays using unique values ranging from 0 through 255. The first 128 values (from 0 through 127) represent the commonly used digits, letters, and punctuation characters. These 128 values are known as the ASCII Standard Character Set. The values 128 through 255 are known as the ASCII Extended Character Set. These characters provide drawing symbols for the IBM PC and

PC-compatible computers. The following table contains the ASCII extended characters:

Sym.	Code	Sym.	Code	Sym.	Code	Sym.	Code
ç	128	á	160	└	192	α	224
ü	129	í	161	┴	193	β	225
é	130	ó	162	┬	194	Γ	226
â	131	ú	163	├	195	π	227
ä	132	ñ	164	—	196	Σ	228
à	133	Ñ	165	┼	197	σ	229
å	134	ª	166	╞	198	μ	230
ç	135	º	167	╟	199	τ	231
ê	136	¿	168	╚	200	Φ	232
ë	137	⌐	169	╔	201	Θ	233
è	138	¬	170	╩	202	Ω	234
ï	139	½	171	╦	203	δ	235
î	140	¼	172	╠	204	∞	236
ì	141	¡	173	═	205	φ	237
Ä	142	«	174	╬	206	ε	238
Å	143	»	175	╧	207	∩	239
É	144	░	176	╨	208	≡	240
æ	145	▓	177	╤	209	±	241
Æ	146	█	178	╥	210	≥	242
ô	147	│	179	╙	211	≤	243
ö	148	┤	180	╘	212	⌠	244
ò	149	╡	181	╒	213	⌡	245
û	150	╢	182	╓	214	÷	246
ù	151	╖	183	╫	215	≈	247
ÿ	152	╕	184	╪	216	°	248
ö	153	╣	185	┘	217	•	249
Ü	154	║	186	┌	218	·	250
¢	155	╗	187	█	219	√	251
£	156	╝	188	▄	220	η	252
¥	157	╜	189	▌	221	²	253
₧	158	╛	190	▐	222	■	254
ƒ	159	┐	191	▀	223	<blank>	255

As you enhance your batch-file capabilities, you might want to enhance your screen display by placing menus and other information within boxes.

Consider a batch file, named BOXMENU.BAT, that displays the following menu:

```
F1 - Display DIRectory listing
F2 - Display DOS version number
F3 - Display disk volume label
F4 - Quit
```

The batch file uses the ASCII extended-character values 179, 191, 192, 196, 217, and 218 to draw the box, as follows:

```
┌218            196            191┐


│179                            179│


└192            196            217┘
```

This batch file can be created using either EDIT (new in DOS 5) or Edlin. As Edlin is supported on all DOS releases, Edlin is used in the following examples. However, users of EDIT can enter the same data as shown on the numbered Edlin text lines, except for the Ctrl–C (displayed as ^C). To begin, enter the ECHO OFF and CLS commands as well as the label :LOOP.

```
C> EDLIN BOXMENU.BAT
New file
*I
        1:* ECHO OFF
        2:* CLS
        3:* :LOOP
        4:*
```

Next, enter ECHO—but do not press Enter. Hold down the Alt key and type *218* (using the numeric keypad at the far right of your keyboard). When you release the Alt key, your screen displays the upper left corner of the box:

```
C> EDLIN BOXMENU.BAT
New file
*I
        1:* ECHO OFF
        2:* CLS
        3:* :LOOP
        4:* ECHO ┌
```

Next, again holding down the Alt key, type *196*. When you release the Alt key, DOS displays a horizontal line segment that extends the top (horizontal) part of the box:

```
C> EDLIN BOXMENU.BAT
New file
*I
        1:* ECHO OFF
        2:* CLS
        3:* :LOOP
        4:* ECHO ┌──
```

Repeat this process until you have typed 35 horizontal lines:

```
C> EDLIN BOXMENU.BAT
New file
*I
        1:* ECHO OFF
        2:* CLS
        3:* :LOOP
        4:* ECHO ┌──────────────────────
```

Complete the top of the box—adding the upper right corner—by holding down the Alt key and typing *191*:

```
C> EDLIN BOXMENU.BAT
New file
*I
        1:* ECHO OFF
        2:* CLS
        3:* :LOOP
        4:* ECHO ┌──────────────────────┐
```

Using the ASCII extended-character value 179 for the vertical bar character, complete the next seven lines as follows:

```
C> EDLIN BOXMENU.BAT
New file
*I
        1:* ECHO OFF
        2:* CLS
        3:* :LOOP
        4:* ECHO
        5:* ECHO     F1 - Display DIRectory listing
        6:* ECHO
        7:* ECHO     F2 - Display DOS version number
        8:* ECHO
        9:* ECHO     F3 - Display disk volume label
       10:* ECHO
       11:* ECHO     F4 - Quit
```

The bottom of the box is much like the top—except that you must use the ASCII extended-character values 192 and 217 for the lower left and lower right corners of the box.

Enter the batch-file commands from the batch file DOSMENU.BAT, which you created earlier. When you do this, BOXMENU.BAT becomes:

```
C> EDLIN BOXMENU.BAT
New file
*I
        1:* ECHO OFF
        2:* CLS
        3:* :LOOP
        4:* ECHO
        5:* ECHO     F1 - Display DIRectory listing
        6:* ECHO
        7:* ECHO     F2 - Display DOS version number
        8:* ECHO
        9:* ECHO     F3 - Display disk volume label
       10:* ECHO
       11:* ECHO     F4 - Quit
       12:* ECHO
       13:* REM Get user response
       14:* :GET_KEY
       15:* F1TOF10
```

```
16:* IF ERRORLEVEL 63 GOTO GET_KEY
17:* IF ERRORLEVEL 62 GOTO DONE
18:* IF ERRORLEVEL 61 IF NOT ERRORLEVEL 62 VOL
19:* IF ERRORLEVEL 60 IF NOT ERRORLEVEL 61 VER
20:* IF ERRORLEVEL 59 IF NOT ERRORLEVEL 60 DIR
21:* GOTO LOOP
22:* :DONE
23:* ^C
```

The ASCII extended character set gives you greatly expanded screen-presentation capabilities. Don't restrict your screens. For example, by adding a few more ECHO commands to the previous batch file, the menu becomes:

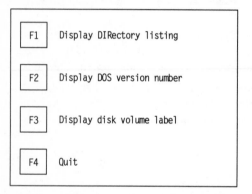

```
F1    Display DIRectory listing

F2    Display DOS version number

F3    Display disk volume label

F4    Quit
```

By now you have put together a powerful collection of batch-processing tools. Show off your skills by developing professional-quality screen displays.

PART IX

Building a Batch-File Library

So far, we have looked at several simple batch files that you might use on a daily basis. In this section, we add four more general-purpose batch procedures. As you work with these batch files, modify them as your needs require.

SETTING SCREEN COLORS

A batch file, named COLORS.BAT, lets you use your keyboard direction keys to cycle through the background screen colors supported by the ANSI.SYS device driver. Each time you press the Up or the Down direction (arrow) key, the batch file changes the screen color. After you press the Enter key, the newly selected color remains active for the remainder of your session.

```
ECHO OFF
REM Allow the user to cycle through the background
REM screen colors that are available, until the user
REM presses Enter to select a color.
SET CURRENT=BLACK
:LOOP
IF %CURRENT%==BLACK ECHO Escape[40m
IF %CURRENT%==RED ECHO Escape[41m
IF %CURRENT%==GREEN ECHO Escape[42m
IF %CURRENT%==YELLOW ECHO Escape[43m
IF %CURRENT%==BLUE ECHO Escape[44m
IF %CURRENT%==MAGENTA ECHO Escape[45m
IF %CURRENT%==CYAN ECHO Escape[46m
IF %CURRENT%==WHITE ECHO Escape[47m
```

```
CLS
ECHO Press Enter to select the current color
ECHO Use the Up and Down arrow keys to change colors
GETARROW
IF ERRORLEVEL 80 GOTO DOWN_ARROW
IF ERRORLEVEL 72 GOTO UP_ARROW
IF ERRORLEVEL 13 GOTO DONE
:DOWN_ARROW
IF NOT %CURRENT%==BLACK GOTO DN_RED
SET CURRENT=RED
GOTO LOOP
:DN_RED
IF NOT %CURRENT%==RED GOTO DN_GREEN
SET CURRENT=GREEN
GOTO LOOP
:DN_GREEN
IF NOT %CURRENT%==GREEN GOTO DN_YELLOW
SET CURRENT=YELLOW
GOTO LOOP
:DN_YELLOW
IF NOT %CURRENT%==YELLOW GOTO DN_BLUE
SET CURRENT=BLUE
GOTO LOOP
:DN_BLUE
IF NOT %CURRENT%==BLUE GOTO DN_MAGENTA
SET CURRENT=MAGENTA
GOTO LOOP
:DN_MAGENTA
IF NOT %CURRENT%==MAGENTA GOTO DN_CYAN
SET CURRENT=CYAN
GOTO LOOP
:DN_CYAN
IF NOT %CURRENT%==CYAN GOTO DN_WHITE
SET CURRENT=WHITE
GOTO LOOP
:DN_WHITE
SET CURRENT=BLACK
GOTO LOOP

:UP_ARROW
IF NOT %CURRENT%==BLACK GOTO UP_RED
SET CURRENT=WHITE
GOTO LOOP
:UP_RED
```

```
IF NOT %CURRENT%==RED GOTO UP_GREEN
SET CURRENT=BLACK
GOTO LOOP
:UP_GREEN
IF NOT %CURRENT%==GREEN GOTO UP_YELLOW
SET CURRENT=RED
GOTO LOOP
:UP_YELLOW
IF NOT %CURRENT%==YELLOW GOTO UP_BLUE
SET CURRENT=GREEN
GOTO LOOP
:UP_BLUE
IF NOT %CURRENT%==BLUE GOTO UP_MAGENTA
SET CURRENT=YELLOW
GOTO LOOP
:UP_MAGENTA
IF NOT %CURRENT%==MAGENTA GOTO UP_CYAN
SET CURRENT=BLUE
GOTO LOOP
:UP_CYAN
IF NOT %CURRENT%==CYAN GOTO UP_WHITE
SET CURRENT=MAGENTA
GOTO LOOP
:UP_WHITE
SET CURRENT=CYAN
GOTO LOOP

:DONE
```

Although long, the COLORS.BAT batch file is simple.
The batch file uses the named parameter CURRENT to
track the current background color. Based on
CURRENT's value, the batch file writes the corresponding ANSI.SYS escape sequence to the screen display.
The batch file uses the program GETARROW.COM,
which we created earlier in this reference using
DEBUG. If you press the Up or the Down direction
(arrow) key, the batch file cycles to the appropriate background color. After you press Enter, the batch file completes execution. As discussed earlier, for this batch file
to successfully execute, you must have previously installed the ANSI.SYS device driver in CONFIG.SYS.

PREVENTING HARD-DISK FORMATTING

Many hard disks have fallen victim to errant FORMAT commands issued by novice users. To prevent this from occurring, many people remove the FORMAT.COM file from a hard disk that is shared by many users. Removing the FORMAT.COM file does eliminate the possibility of the user accidently formatting the hard disk, but it also removes a necessary DOS command. If users are doing serious work on a hard-disk system, eventually they will want to copy that work to floppy disks. To do so, the users will probably have to format floppy disks.

As an alternate solution, you can rename the DOS command FORMAT to FMAT.COM. Next, create a batch file, named FORMAT.BAT, that contains the following:

```
ECHO OFF
IF "%1"=="" GOTO NO_PARAMS
ECHO To prevent inadvertent formatting of the hard
ECHO disk, this batch file lets you format only
ECHO floppy disks in drive A or B. Specify the disk
ECHO drive to use in your command line.
ECHO Example: FORMAT A:
ECHO Do you want to continue (Y/N)?
GETYORN
IF ERRORLEVEL 89 GOTO CONTINUE_FORMAT
IF ERRORLEVEL 78 GOTO DONE
:CONTINUE_FORMAT
IF "%1"=="" GOTO NO_PARAMS
IF "%1"=="A:" GOTO VALID_DRIVE
IF "%1"=="B:" GOTO VALID_DRIVE
GOTO INVALID_DRIVE
:NO_PARAMS
ECHO You must specify the disk drive to format
ECHO in your command line.
GOTO DONE
:VALID_DRIVE
FMAT %1 %2 %3 %4 %5 %6 %7 %8 %9
GOTO DONE
:INVALID_DRIVE
ECHO This batch file formats only disks in
ECHO drive A or B. The batch file considers
```

```
ECHO the disk drive %1 invalid.
:DONE
```

This batch file lets users format only floppy disks in either drive A or drive B. When you run this batch file, DOS displays:

```
To prevent inadvertent formatting of the hard
disk, this batch file lets you format only
floppy disks in drive A or B. Specify the disk
drive to use in your command line.
Example: FORMAT A:
Do you want to continue (Y/N)?
```

If you press Y to continue the batch file, the batch file tests whether you are trying to format a disk in a drive other than A or B. If so, the batch file displays an error message and stops. If you are formatting a disk in drive A or drive B, the batch file executes FMAT.COM using all the batch parameters.

Remember: In some cases, the FORMAT command line requires additional parameters, such as /S or /4. By using %2 through %9, the batch file supports these additional parameters.

GETTING CHARACTER-STRING INPUT

Throughout this reference you have created programs using DEBUG that allow the user to press Y or N for a yes or no response, to enter a specific function key, and to press the Up and Down direction keys. In some cases, however, you might need to get several characters from a user, such as a filename or a password that controls which users can execute a batch file.

The following batch file, named GETPASS.BAT, prompts the user to enter a password. This batch file then compares the user password with the predefined password MANAGEMENT. If the two passwords are identical, the batch file continues processing; otherwise, the batch file displays an error message and stops processing:

```
ECHO OFF
IF NOT EXIST PASSWORD.SET GOTO NO_FILE
```

```
ECHO Enter your password, press F6, and then
ECHO press Enter.
COPY CON PASSWORD.DAT > NUL
COPY PASSWORD.SET+PASSWORD.DAT PASSWORD.BAT > NUL
CALL PASSWORD
IF NOT "%PASSWORD%"=="MANAGEMENT" GOTO BAD_PASSWORD
ECHO Valid password  —     ready to process payroll
GOTO DONE
:NO_FILE
ECHO This batch file requires the file PASSWORD.SET,
ECHO which contains SET PASSWORD=^Z, as discussed
ECHO in the batch-processing reference.
GOTO DONE
:BAD_PASSWORD
ECHO Invalid password
:DONE
SET PASSWORD=
DEL PASSWORD.BAT
DEL PASSWORD.DAT
```

The batch file relies on the file PASSWORD.SET, which
you can create from the DOS prompt. To begin, issue the
following command, as follows:

```
C> COPY CON PASSWORD.SET
```

Next, type *SET PASSWORD=*, but do not press Enter. Instead, immediately following the equal sign, press the F6
function key and then press Enter. When you do so, DOS
creates the file PASSWORD.SET, as follows:

```
C> COPY CON PASSWORD.SET
SET PASSWORD=^Z
        1 File(s) copied

C>
```

When you run the batch file GETPASS.BAT, it prompts
you to enter a password:

```
Enter your password, press F6, and then
press Enter.
```

At this prompt, type *MANAGEMENT*, press F6, and then press Enter. When you do so, the batch file copies the information you type into the file PASSWORD.DAT. The command:

```
COPY CON PASSWORD.DAT > NUL
```

directs DOS to copy information from the keyboard into the file PASSWORD.DAT until you press F6 to signify the end of the file. The command redirects the message:

```
    1 File(s) copied
```

to the NUL device so that the message does not appear on your screen.

Next, the command:

```
COPY PASSWORD.SET+PASSWORD.DAT PASSWORD.BAT > NUL
```

directs DOS to append the contents of PASSWORD.DAT to the contents of the file PASSWORD.SET, creating the batch file PASSWORD.BAT. Assuming that you previously typed the password MANAGEMENT, the file PASSWORD.BAT now contains:

```
SET PASSWORD=MANAGEMENT
```

GETPASS.BAT then runs the PASSWORD.BAT batch file, which creates the named parameter PASSWORD in the DOS environment. After this entry exists, the batch file can compare the password with MANAGEMENT using the IF batch command. If the passwords differ, the batch file displays an error message and stops processing. If the passwords are the same, the batch file can execute its protected commands. Notice that, before completing execution, the batch file removes the PASSWORD environment entry as well as the files PASSWORD.BAT and PASSWORD.DAT.

Admittedly, you probably won't need to get a password for many batch-file applications. This batch file was presented to teach you how to perform user input from within your batch files.

SIMPLIFYING YOUR SYSTEM-BACKUP OPERATIONS

A batch file, named FILEBU.BAT, helps you perform disk-backup operations. When you run this batch file, DOS displays:

```
F1 - Monthly Backup
F2 - Daily/Incremental Backup
F3 - Specific Files Backup
F4 - Quit
```

If you press the F1 function key, the batch file performs a monthly backup. A monthly backup is a backup of every file on your disk. Depending on the number of files on your disk, a monthly backup can be quite time-consuming. If you press the F2 function key, the batch file performs an incremental backup, backing up only those files that have been created or modified since the last system backup. (An incremental backup can be much faster than a system backup.) You must, however, keep all your incremental backup disks from one system backup to another. This ensures that you have a copy of every file on your disk.

If you press the F3 function key, the batch file prompts you to enter the file specifications for the files to back up as well as for the target disk drive. To back up all the files in the subdirectory DOS to the floppy disk in drive A, for example, you would enter:

```
C> C:\DOS    A:
```

Next, you must press the F6 function key and then press Enter. The batch file will back up only the files you specify.

If you press the F4 key, the batch file stops processing.

For ease of understanding, view this batch file as though it were four distinct batch files—FILEBU.BAT, MONTHLY.BAT, DAILY.BAT, and SPECIFIC.BAT.

The batch file FILEBU.BAT contains:

```
ECHO OFF
REM Allow the user to perform a monthly, daily, or
REM specific file backup.
CLS
```

```
REM Loop until the user presses the F4 key to quit.
:LOOP
ECHO F1 - Monthly Backup
ECHO F2 - Daily/Incremental Backup
ECHO F3 - Specific Files Backup
ECHO F4 - Quit
REM Get user response.
:GET_KEY
F1TOF10
REM If user presses a key other than F1 to F4, get
REM another key.
IF ERRORLEVEL 63 GOTO GET_KEY
IF ERRORLEVEL 62 GOTO DONE
IF ERRORLEVEL 61 IF NOT ERRORLEVEL 62 CALL SPECIFIC
IF ERRORLEVEL 60 IF NOT ERRORLEVEL 61 CALL DAILY
IF ERRORLEVEL 59 IF NOT ERRORLEVEL 60 CALL MONTHLY
GOTO LOOP
:DONE
```

As you can see, this batch file displays the main menu and then uses a program, named F1TOF10.COM, to get a function key from the user. Depending on the function key pressed, the batch file calls either MONTHLY.BAT for a complete disk backup, DAILY.BAT for an incremental backup, or SPECIFIC.BAT for a specific file backup. The batch file continues to loop, repeating this process until the user presses the F4 key to quit.

The batch file MONTHLY.BAT performs a complete disk-backup operation. When you select this option, DOS displays:

```
The monthly backup copies all the files on
your hard disk to a floppy disk.

Depending on the number of files on your disk,
the monthly backup can be quite time-consuming.
Do you wish to continue (Y/N)?
```

This message simply explains the monthly backup procedures and lets the user continue or cancel the operation. If the user responds by pressing Y to continue the operation, the DOS command BACKUP backs up the entire disk to floppy disks in drive A:

```
REM Perform a complete backup of the system disk.
ECHO The monthly backup copies all the files on
```

```
ECHO your hard disk to a floppy disk.

ECHO Depending on the number of files on your disk,
ECHO the monthly backup can be quite time-consuming.
ECHO Do you wish to continue (Y/N)?
GETYORN
IF ERRORLEVEL 89 GOTO BACKUP
IF ERRORLEVEL 78 GOTO RETURN
:BACKUP
ECHO Be sure that you label each disk with the
ECHO current date, the words MONTHLY BACKUP, and
ECHO your initials.
BACKUP C:\*.*  A:  /S
:RETURN
CLS
```

The batch file DAILY.BAT is very similar to the batch file
MONTHLY.BAT:

```
REM Perform a backup of each file on the disk changed
REM or created since the last system backup.

ECHO The daily backup copies all the files on
ECHO your hard disk that have been changed or created
ECHO since the last BACKUP to floppy.
ECHO
ECHO Do you wish to continue (Y/N)?
GETYORN
IF ERRORLEVEL 89 GOTO BACKUP
IF ERRORLEVEL 78 GOTO RETURN
:BACKUP
ECHO Be sure that you label each disk with the
ECHO current date, the words DAILY BACKUP, and
ECHO your initials. Use the disk from the previous
ECHO daily backup until the floppy fills.
BACKUP C:\*.*  A:  /S /A /M
:RETURN
CLS
```

As you can see, if the user responds by pressing Y to continue the batch file, the BACKUP command executes an
incremental backup of the files on the disk.

Of the four backup batch files, the batch file SPECIFIC.BAT
is the most interesting. This batch file lets the user type the

names of the files that are to be backed up. SPECIFIC.BAT
depends on a file, named BACKUP.FMT, that you can create
at the DOS prompt:

```
REM Back up one or more user-specified files to disk.
REM Prompt the user to enter the filename to back up.
REM Copy the names to the file BACKUP.DAT. Using the
REM file BACKUP.FMT, create a BACKUP command in the
REM batch file BACKIT.BAT.
IF NOT EXIST BACKUP.FMT GOTO NO_FORMAT
ECHO The specific-file option allows you to back up
ECHO one or more files.
ECHO Do you want to continue (Y/N)?
GETYORN
IF ERRORLEVEL 89 GOTO BACKUP
IF ERRORLEVEL 78 GOTO RETURN
NO_FORMAT:
ECHO The specific-file backup requires the file
ECHO BACKUP.FMT, which contains BACKUP ^Z, as
ECHO discussed in the batch-file reference.
PAUSE
GOTO RETURN
:BACKUP
ECHO Type the file specification to backup and
ECHO the target disk-drive identification,
ECHO press the F6 key, and then press Enter.
ECHO Example: *.DAT A: ^Z [Enter]
COPY CON BACKUP.DAT > NUL
COPY BACKUP.FMT+BACKUP.DAT BACKIT.BAT
CALL BACKIT
DEL BACKUP.DAT
DEL BACKIT.BAT
:RETURN
CLS
```

Using the COPY CON BACKUP.FMT command, begin
the file copy:

```
C> COPY CON BACKUP.FMT
```

Type *BACKUP* followed by a space, and press F6 to mark
the end of the file:

```
C> COPY CON BACKUP.FMT
BACKUP ^Z
```

When you press Enter, DOS creates the file, as follows:

```
C> COPY CON BACKUP.FMT
BACKUP ^Z
        1 File(s) copied

C>
```

(If the batch file should ever discover that the file
BACKUP.FMT does not exist, the batch file displays an
error message and returns to the main menu.)

Assuming that the file BACKUP.FMT does exist, if you
press Y to continue the batch file, the batch file prompts
you to type the filename to backup as well as the target
disk drive:

```
Type the file specification to backup and
the target disk-drive identification,
press the F6 key, and then press Enter.
Example: *.DAT A: ^Z [Enter]
```

The batch file places the information you type into the file
BACKUP.DAT. By redirecting its output to the NUL device, the command:

```
COPY CON BACKUP.DAT > NUL
```

suppresses the display of the message:

```
        1 File(s) copied
```

Next, the command:

```
COPY BACKUP.FMT+BACKUP.DAT BACKIT.BAT
```

appends the contents of the file BACKUP.DAT (which
contains the filename to back up) to the file
BACKUP.FMT (which contains the BACKUP command).
The resulting file is a batch file, named BACKIT.BAT,
that the batch file runs next. Assuming the user types
C:\DOS and then types *A:*, the file BACKIT.BAT contains:

```
BACKUP C:\DOS A:
```

As you can see, the command backs up only the subdirectory desired. When the BACKUP command completes execution, the batch file deletes the files BACKUP.DAT and
BACKIT.BAT, cleaning up after itself.

The collection of batch files that perform the various backup operations shows you how easy it is to develop powerful utilities using DOS batch files. If you want to enhance these batch files, you might consider using the ANSI.SYS device driver to add color. If you are using DOS version 3.30 or later, you also might want to add the /L qualifier to the BACKUP command, which directs BACKUP to create a log file. Also, you might consider adding exit-status checks using IF ERRORLEVEL to display error messages to the user if BACKUP fails.

PART X

Getting the Most from AUTOEXEC.BAT

CUSTOMIZING AUTOEXEC.BAT

Now that you have seen all the DOS batch-file commands, learned how to create programs using DEBUG, and created several complex batch files, let's take a look at a few fun batch files that you might want to run from your AUTOEXEC.BAT file. All the batch files in this section use a simple program that you can create with DEBUG.

A batch file, named GREETING.BAT, uses the program WEEKDAY.COM to determine the current day of the week. The batch file then displays a message that is appropriate for that day. Here is the batch file:

```
ECHO OFF
REM Determine the day of the week using the program
REM WEEKDAY.COM. The program returns a status value
REM that you can check, using the IF ERRORLEVEL
REM condition. Sunday has the value 0, Monday has the
REM value 1, and so on. Saturday has the value 6.
REM After the batch file determines the day, it
REM displays an appropriate message.
WEEKDAY
IF ERRORLEVEL 0 IF NOT ERRORLEVEL 1 GOTO SUNDAY
IF ERRORLEVEL 1 IF NOT ERRORLEVEL 2 GOTO MONDAY
IF ERRORLEVEL 2 IF NOT ERRORLEVEL 3 GOTO TUESDAY
IF ERRORLEVEL 3 IF NOT ERRORLEVEL 4 GOTO WEDNESDAY
IF ERRORLEVEL 4 IF NOT ERRORLEVEL 5 GOTO THURSDAY
IF ERRORLEVEL 5 IF NOT ERRORLEVEL 6 GOTO FRIDAY
```

```
IF ERRORLEVEL 6 GOTO SATURDAY
:SUNDAY
ECHO It's Sunday — Relax and watch football.
GOTO DONE
:MONDAY
ECHO It's Monday — Get ready for a new week.
GOTO DONE
:TUESDAY
ECHO It's Tuesday — Week is just beginning.
GOTO DONE
:WEDNESDAY
ECHO It's Wednesday — Hump day!
GOTO DONE
:THURSDAY
ECHO It's Thursday — Almost there!
GOTO DONE
:FRIDAY
ECHO It's finally Friday — Happy Hour!
GOTO DONE
:SATURDAY
ECHO It's Saturday — You should be in bed.
:DONE
```

If you have appointments that fall on specific days or a critical meeting that you don't want to forget, you can simply modify the appropriate ECHO statement to remind you about it—either on the day of the meeting or on the day before it. The program, named WEEKDAY.COM, uses the DOS Get Date service to determine the day of the week. The program returns an exit-status value of 0 for Sunday, 1 for Monday, and so on. You can create WEEKDAY.COM using DEBUG, as follows:

```
C> DEBUG WEEKDAY.COM
File not found

-A 100
2AF5:0100 MOV AH, 2A
2AF5:0102 INT 21
2AF5:0104 MOV AH, 4C
2AF5:0106 INT 21
2AF5:0108
-R CX
CX 0000
```

```
:8
-W
Writing 0008 bytes
-Q

C>
```

In a similar manner, the batch file SCHEDULE.BAT
uses a program, named GETMONTH.COM, to determine the current month. After the batch file knows the
month, it branches to commands specific to the month
and displays a list of dates and meetings:

```
ECHO OFF
REM Determine the current month using the program
REM GETMONTH.COM. The program returns a status value
REM from 1 through 12 that represents the current
REM month. (January is 1; December is 12.) After the
REM month is determined, branch to the specified
REM month and display important dates for the month.

GETMONTH
IF ERRORLEVEL  1 IF NOT ERRORLEVEL  2 GOTO JANUARY
IF ERRORLEVEL  2 IF NOT ERRORLEVEL  3 GOTO FEBRUARY
IF ERRORLEVEL  3 IF NOT ERRORLEVEL  4 GOTO MARCH
IF ERRORLEVEL  4 IF NOT ERRORLEVEL  5 GOTO APRIL
IF ERRORLEVEL  5 IF NOT ERRORLEVEL  6 GOTO MAY
IF ERRORLEVEL  6 IF NOT ERRORLEVEL  7 GOTO JUNE
IF ERRORLEVEL  7 IF NOT ERRORLEVEL  8 GOTO JULY
IF ERRORLEVEL  8 IF NOT ERRORLEVEL  9 GOTO AUGUST
IF ERRORLEVEL  9 IF NOT ERRORLEVEL 10 GOTO SEPTEMBER
IF ERRORLEVEL 10 IF NOT ERRORLEVEL 11 GOTO OCTOBER
IF ERRORLEVEL 11 IF NOT ERRORLEVEL 12 GOTO NOVEMBER
IF ERRORLEVEL 12 GOTO DECEMBER


:JANUARY
ECHO January  1 - New Year's Day
ECHO January 15 - Martin Luther King's Birthday
GOTO DONE

:FEBRUARY
ECHO February 12 - Lincoln's Birthday
ECHO February 14 - Valentine's Day
ECHO February 22 - Washington's Birthday
GOTO DONE
```

```
:MARCH
ECHO March 17 - St. Patrick's Day
GOTO DONE

:APRIL
ECHO April 1 - April Fools' Day
GOTO DONE

:MAY
ECHO May 1 - May Day
ECHO Last Monday in May - Memorial Day
GOTO DONE

:JUNE
GOTO DONE

:JULY
ECHO July 4 - Independence Day
GOTO DONE

:AUGUST
GOTO DONE

:SEPTEMBER
ECHO First Monday in September - Labor Day
GOTO DONE

:OCTOBER
ECHO October 12 - Columbus Day
ECHO October 31 - Halloween
GOTO DONE

:NOVEMBER
ECHO November 11 - Veterans' Day
ECHO Fourth Thursday - Thanksgiving Day
GOTO DONE

:DECEMBER
ECHO Hanukkah begins
ECHO December 25 - Christmas

:DONE
```

In this case, the batch file contains several of the major holidays. Using the ECHO command, you can easily add birthdays, anniversaries, or other important dates. You can create the program GETMONTH.COM using DEBUG, as follows:

```
C> DEBUG GETMONTH.COM
File not found

-A 100
2AF5:0100 MOV AH, 2A
2AF5:0102 INT 21
2AF5:0104 MOV AL, DH
2AF5:0106 MOV AH, 4C
2AF5:0108 INT 21
2AF5:010A
-R CX
CX 0000
:A
-W
Writing 000A bytes
-Q

C>
```

In some cases, your batch processing might be specific to a day of the month, such as the 15th. The following program, named GETDAY.COM, returns an exit-status value that contains the day of the month:

```
C> DEBUG GETDAY.COM
File not found

-A 100
2AF5:0100 MOV AH, 2A
2AF5:0102 INT 21
2AF5:0104 MOV AL, DL
2AF5:0106 MOV AH, 4C
2AF5:0108 INT 21
2AF5:010A
-R CX
CX 0000
:A
-W
Writing 000A bytes
-Q

C>
```

The following two commands show you how to determine the 15th after your batch file runs GETDAY.COM:

```
GETDAY
IF ERRORLEVEL 15 IF NOT ERRORLEVEL 16 GOTO 15TH
```

Many users like to delete old and unneeded copies of their files on a specific date. Using the GETDAY.COM program, AUTOEXEC.BAT determines if today is the day to delete files and, if it is, deletes the files.

A batch file, named GETTIME.BAT, uses a program, named GETHOUR.COM, to determine the current hour.

The batch file then displays a message to the user, such as *Good Morning*, based on the current time:

```
ECHO OFF
REM Determine the current hour of the day using the
REM GETHOUR.COM program. GETHOUR returns a status
REM value from 0 to 23. (0 is midnight, 1 is 1AM,
REM 12 is noon, 13 is 1PM, and so on.) After the
REM hour is known, display a specified message
REM to the user.

GETHOUR

IF ERRORLEVEL  0 IF NOT ERRORLEVEL 6 GOTO TOO_LATE
IF ERRORLEVEL  6 IF NOT ERRORLEVEL 12 GOTO MORNING
IF ERRORLEVEL 12 IF NOT ERRORLEVEL 18 GOTO AFTERNOON
IF ERRORLEVEL 18 GOTO EVENING

:TOO_LATE
ECHO You're up either too late or too early.
GOTO DONE

:MORNING
ECHO Good Morning.
GOTO DONE

:AFTERNOON
ECHO Good Afternoon.
GOTO DONE
```

```
:EVENING
ECHO Good Evening. It's starting to get late.

:DONE
```

A program, named GETHOUR.COM, uses the DOS Get Time service to determine the current hour. You can create this program using DEBUG, as follows:

```
C> DEBUG GETHOUR.COM
File not found

-A 100
2AF5:0100 MOV AH, 2C
2AF5:0102 INT 21
2AF5:0104 MOV AL, CH
2AF5:0106 MOV AH, 4C
2AF5:0108 INT 21
2AF5:010A
-R CX
CX 0000
:A
-W
Writing 000A bytes
-Q

C>
```

In a similar manner, a program, named GETMIN.COM, returns the minutes of the current time:

```
C> DEBUG GETMIN.COM
File not found

-A 100
2AF5:0100 MOV AH, 2C
2AF5:0102 INT 21
2AF5:0104 MOV AL, CL
2AF5:0106 MOV AH, 4C
2AF5:0108 INT 21
2AF5:010A
-R CX
CX 0000
:A
-W
Writing 000A bytes
-Q

C>
```

With these tools in hand, you can unleash the power of your batch files. Change these batch files as your needs change. Experiment with the programs presented in this section; I think you will enjoy using them.

PART XI
Appendixes

APPENDIX A:
SUMMARY OF DOS EXIT-STATUS VALUES

Several DOS commands provide exit-status values that you can test using IF ERRORLEVEL. The following table lists each exit value that DOS provides:

Command	Error Status	Meaning
BACKUP	0	Successful backup
BACKUP	1	No files to back up
BACKUP	2	File-sharing conflict, backup incomplete
BACKUP	3	User Ctrl-C, backup incomplete
BACKUP	4	Fatal error, backup incomplete
DISKCOMP	0	Disks compared exactly
DISKCOMP	1	Disks were not the same
DISKCOMP	2	User Ctrl-C, diskcomp incomplete
DISKCOMP	3	Unrecoverable read or write error
DISKCOMP	4	Insufficient memory, invalid drive, or syntax error
DISKCOPY	0	Copy was successful
DISKCOPY	1	Nonfatal read or write error
DISKCOPY	2	User Ctrl-C, diskcopy incomplete
DISKCOPY	3	Unable to either read source disk or format target disk
DISKCOPY	4	Insufficient memory, invalid drive, or syntax error
FORMAT	0	Successful format
FORMAT	3	User Ctrl-C, format incomplete

(continued)

continued

Command	Error Status	Meaning
FORMAT	4	Fatal error, format incomplete
FORMAT	5	User pressed N at continue prompt
GRAFTABL	0	Command successful
GRAFTABL	1	Previously loaded table replaced
GRAFTABL	2	No new table loaded
GRAFTABL	3	Invalid command-line parameter
GRAFTABL	4	Incorrect DOS version
KEYB	0	Successful keyboard load
KEYB	1	Invalid command line
KEYB	2	Invalid keyboard definition table
KEYB	3	Cannot create table
KEYB	4	CON device error
KEYB	5	Code page not prepared
KEYB	6	Missing translation table
KEYB	7	Incorrect DOS version
REPLACE	0	Successful replacement
REPLACE	2	Source file not found
REPLACE	3	Source or target path not found
REPLACE	5	Read-only target file
REPLACE	8	Insufficient memory
REPLACE	11	Invalid command line
REPLACE	15	Invalid disk drive specification
REPLACE	22*	Incorrect version of DOS
RESTORE	0	Successful restore
RESTORE	1	No files found
RESTORE	2*	File-sharing conflict, restore incomplete
RESTORE	3	User Ctrl-C, restore incomplete
RESTORE	4	Fatal error, restore incomplete

*MS-DOS does not return this code.

MS-DOS version 5.0 provides the following:

Command	Error Status	Meaning
SETVER	0	Successful completion
SETVER	1	Invalid command line switch
SETVER	2	Invalid file name specified
SETVER	3	Insufficient memory
SETVER	4	Invalid version number specified
SETVER	5	Entry specified not found in table
SETVER	6	MS-DOS system files not found
SETVER	7	Invalid drive specified
SETVER	8	Too many command line parameters
SETVER	9	Missing command line parameter
SETVER	10	Error reading MS-DOS system files
SETVER	11	Version table is corrupted in MS-DOS system files
SETVER	12	MS-DOS system files don't support a version table
SETVER	13	Insufficient space in version table
SETVER	14	Error writing to MS-DOS system files

MS-DOS 4.0 and later provide the following:

Command	Error Status*	Meaning
XCOPY	0	Copy without error
XCOPY	1	No files found to copy
XCOPY	2	Ctrl-C, XCOPY incomplete
XCOPY	4	Initialization error (not enough memory, invalid drive, file or path not found, or command-line syntax error)
XCOPY	5	Int 24 Error occurred

*PC-DOS does not return these codes.

APPENDIX B:
SUMMARY OF ANSI.SYS COMMANDS

Throughout this reference, we have made extensive use of
ANSI.SYS escape sequences. The following table summa-
rizes the ANSI.SYS commands:

Sequence	Function
Escape[*rows*A	Moves cursor up the number of rows speci-fied.
Escape[*rows*B	Moves cursor down the number of rows specified.
Escape[*rows*C	Moves cursor right the number of rows specified.
Escape[*rows*D	Moves cursor left the number of rows spec-ified.
Escape[*row*;*col*H	Moves cursor to row and column position.
Escape[*row*;*col*f	(Same as Escape[*row*;*col*H.)
Escape[*row*;*col*R	Reports current row and column. (Note: MS-DOS does not support this sequence.)
Escape[s	Saves cursor position.
Escape[u	Restores cursor position.
Escape[2J	Clears screen display. Places cursor at home position.
Escape[K	Erases to end of line.
Escape[*color*m	Sets screen-color attribute.
Escape[6n	Reports console device status.
Escape[=*mode*l*	Resets video mode.
Escape[=*mode*h	Sets video mode.
Escape[=7l*	Disables line wrap.
Escape[0;*fkey*; "string"p	Defines a function key.
Escape[0q†	Ignores commands that attempt to assign additional keys on enhanced keyboard.
Escape[1q†‡	Allows additional keys on enhanced key-board to be assigned, even though ANSI.SYS was loaded without the / X switch.

*Note that the last character is the lowercase *l* (not the uppercase *I* or the
digit *1*).
†New with PC-DOS version 4.0; not available in MS-DOS.
‡Note that the value is the digit one (not lowercase *l*), followed by lowercase *q*.

Index

Special Characters

$ metacharacters 20–21, 112

% parameters 56–57, 73–74, 85, 97–100

* wildcard character or Edlin prompt 12, 56, 74, 112

: batch label 80

== equality of character strings 62–64

DOS prompt 20–21, 25, 26, 111

? wildcard character 74

@ character and command name suppression 30–32, 43

  redirecting output with 36

^G ASCII bell sound 44–45

^V[ASCII escape character 123, 124

^Z end of file marker 9

- DEBUG prompt 130

A

A100 DEBUG command 130

Alternate (Alt) key

  ASCII characters and 147–49

  bell sound, creating 43–46

  blank lines, creating 51–52, 82

ANSI.SYS device driver 116–28

  blinking characters, displaying 119–20

  color values, supported by 117–18, 151–53

  command summary 175

  cursor, controlling with 124

  escape sequences 117–23

  help text, displaying 125–26

ANSI.SYS device driver, *continued*

  installing 116–17

  keys, redefining with 126–28

  named parameters 120–22

  screen colors, setting with 119–20

  screen display, erasing 122–23

ARROW. BAT file 143–45

ASCII characters

  Alternate keys and 147–49

  bell sound 43–46

  blank line, displaying, using ECHO 50, 82

  drawing symbols, and 145–50

  escape sequences 117–19, 122–23

  standard set 145

ASCII extended character set and definitions 50, 127–28, 145–50

ASCII nondocument mode, saving batch files in 103

AUTOEXEC.BAT file 30–32

  changing contents of, when installing software packages 88–89

  vs CONFIG.SYS 26–28

  customizing 164–71

  DATE command 26

  DOS commands, executing with 23–26

  ECHO OFF command 32

  keys, redefining with ANSI.SYS 127

  macros, installing 112

  PAUSE command 60–61

177

KRIS JAMSA

Kris Jamsa graduated from the United States Air Force Academy with a degree in computer science in 1983. He moved to Las Vegas, Nevada, where he began work as a VAX/VMS system manager for the U.S. Air Force. In 1986 Jamsa received a master's degree in computer science (with an emphasis in operating systems) from the University of Nevada at Las Vegas. He taught computer science at the National University in San Diego, California, for one year before leaving the Air Force in 1988 to begin writing full-time. He is the author of more than a dozen books on DOS, OS/2, Windows, hard-disk management, and the Pascal and C programming languages. With Microsoft Press, Jamsa has published *Microsoft QuickPascal Programming*; *Graphics Programming with Microsoft C and Microsoft QuickC*; *Microsoft C: Secrets, Shortcuts, and Solutions*; and numerous quick references. Jamsa resides in Las Vegas with his wife and their two daughters.

The manuscript for this book was prepared and submitted to Microsoft Press in electronic form. Text files were processed and formatted using Microsoft Word.

Principal word processor: Sigrid Wile
Principal proofreader: Carmen Wiseman
Principal typographer: Michelle Neil
Interior text designer: Darcie S. Furlan
Cover designer: Celeste Design
Cover color separator: Rainier Color

Text composition by Editorial Services of New England, Inc. in Times Roman with display type in Futura Heavy, using Xerox Ventura Publisher and the Compugraphic 9600.